Albert Peter Low, James Melville Macoun

Report of the Mistassini Expedition 1884-5

Albert Peter Low, James Melville Macoun

Report of the Mistassini Expedition 1884-5

ISBN/EAN: 9783337329945

Printed in Europe, USA, Canada, Australia, Japan

Cover: Foto ©Andreas Hilbeck / pixelio.de

More available books at **www.hansebooks.com**

GEOLOGICAL AND NATURAL HISTORY SURVEY OF CANADA
ALFRED R. C. SELWYN, LL.D., F.R.S., F.G.S., DIRECTOR.

REPORT

OF THE

MISTASSINI EXPEDITION.

1884-5.

BY

A. P. LOW, B.Ap.Sc.

PUBLISHED BY AUTHORITY OF PARLIAMENT.

MONTREAL:
DAWSON BROTHERS.
1885.

ALFRED R. C. SELWYN, LL.D., F.R.S., etc.,

Director Geological and Natural History Survey of Canada.

SIR,—I herewith beg to submit my report of the Mistassini Expedition of 1884 and 1885.

I may take this opportunity of acknowledging the help kindly afforded me by all the officers of the Hudson Bay Company with whom I had the pleasure to come in contact.

I am,

Sir,

Your humble servant.

A. P. LOW.

REPORT

OF THE

MISTASSINI EXPEDITION,

1884–5.

BY

A. P. LOW, B.Ap.Sc.

According to instructions, I left Ottawa June 9th. 1884, to join the Mistassini Expedition, then being fitted out in Quebec, and reported there, June 12th, to Mr. John Bignell, in charge. I remained in Quebec, awaiting the departure of the party, until July 19th, when we proceeded to Rimouski, and were there again obliged to wait for the schooner engaged to transport the outfit from Quebec to Betsiamites, which did not arrive at Rimouski until the 25th, when we crossed to Betsiamites or Bersimis.

On account of further delay in engaging Indians and preparing the outfit, it was not until August 8th that I started, with one canoe and two men, up the Betsiamites River, in advance of the main party, for the purpose of making an examination of the rocks along the river as far as Lake Pipmuakin, where Mr. Bignell was to commence his survey.

Betsiamites or Bersimis River.

We proceeded up the river and reached the first fall on the 11th, the distance being about forty-five miles in a north-west course. The river has been navigated to this point by a small steamer belonging to the lumber mill situated at its mouth.

The river valley, cut in the surrounding table-land, varies from a quarter of a mile to one mile in width. Its sides are formed by Laurentian hills, elevated from two to six hundred feet above the stream. These hills are well wooded with white and black spruce, tamarac, balsam-poplar and birch, and quantities of valuable timber are taken out every year, and cut up by the steam mill at the mouth of the river. The valley has been partly filled up by deposits of glacial drift, as the banks of the river are, for the most part, of sand

Timber.

and clay, often upwards of fifty feet high. Much of the clay shows distinct evidence of stratification, and the different beds are seen highly crumpled and folded.

Between these banks, the river, varying from one to two hundred yards in breadth, flows with a swift and even current, and is joined by a number of small streams on either side, the chief one being the Neepee River, which flows from the eastward and joins the main stream at the head of tide, seven miles from the sea. This tributary descends into the valley by a beautiful fall, over 100 feet high.

Forest fires.

About thirty miles up the river and northwards, the country has been traversed by frequent and extensive fires, which have left very little of the original forest, the region being, for the most part, covered with second-growth timber of aspen-poplar, white birch, banksian pine, and spruce, none of which has attained a large size. The first fall is formed by two chutes, each being about fifty feet high, with a whirlpool between them, into which a large number of logs have, from time to time, been carried, and before escaping from its influence, having been so broken and bruised as to be unfit for commercial purposes, remain piled up on the shore. Above this fall the river runs N. 30° W., and continues in this direction for ten miles, with a sluggish current. The hills on either side rise to elevations from 800 to 1,000 feet above its level, being for the most part bare or covered with small second-growth timber.

The river now flows from the west for nine miles, in the lower four of which it is very rough, having four chutes of fifteen, ten, ten and twenty feet, respectively, with strong rapids between them, necessitating a portage of canoes for that distance.

From here to Waweashton, distant ten miles, the course is N. 35° W., with two short portages, passing falls of twelve and thirty feet.

Long Portage.

At Waweashton a large branch comes in from the eastward: and the main stream, turning westward, falls in the next ten miles fully 500 feet from the general plateau into the river valley, and is quite impassable for canoes, so that a portage, over a mountain upwards of 1,000 feet high, must be made. A week was spent transporting canoes, provisions, etc., over this distance. Beyond this, the river turns to the north, and for sixteen miles widens out into Lake Natuakimin, with a width of from one-half to one and a-half miles; lying very little below the general surface of the surrounding country, which is here comparatively flat, and characterized by low hills only, which seldom rise more than 200 feet above the water-level.

The river next runs from the west for fifteen miles, having become narrow and rapid, with a mile and a-half portage at the end of the course. The banks and country are similar to those on the last course.

Next turning to the north-east, the river, for a distance of eight miles, breaks in a straight line through the Labradorite hills, which form almost vertical walls on either side, rising from two to four hundred feet above the water, and producing the finest scenery met with on this route. Above this is Lake Pipmuakin, which was reached August 25th, and is distant by the river 135 miles from the sea.

This lake is very irregular in shape, being full of deep bays, and has an area of over 100 square miles. The Betsiamites River flows through it on the east side, the distance between inlet and outlet being nine miles. Several other smaller rivers and numerous brooks also empty into the lake. Lake Pipmuakin.

The shores of the lake are principally low, but in places are rocky, and rise in elevations of one to two hundred feet above the water, the whole being covered with a fair growth of white spruce, balsam-spruce and white birch.

The waters of the lake and the Betsiamites River are well stocked with fish, the principal kinds being lake- and river-trout, white-fish, pike and sucker, and below the first fall of the river, salmon and sea-trout.

Mr. Bignell having arrived at this lake on September 10th, the party was again divided, Mr. Bignell, with two canoes and four men, going by the Betsiamites River to Lake Manouan, by way of Lake Manouanis, while I, with five canoes and eight men, proceeded to the same point by a portage route to the Manouan River, and up that river to the lake. Arrival of Mr. Bignell.

Leaving Mr. Bignell, September 15th, we proceeded by a bay running to the north-west, to Pipmuakin River, a small stream discharging into the lake at the head of the bay, and distant twenty miles from the outlet. In crossing the lake, we were much delayed by wind, and did not reach the river until the 19th.

Having proceeded up the Pipmuakin River, through low, swampy country, a distance of twelve miles, the general course being N. 15° W., we left it, and, passing over four portages and three smaller lakes,) the total distance being five miles, direction north-west,) we reached a small lake called Otăshoao, which discharges, by a small river two miles long, into the Manouan River. This river is a branch of the Peribonka, which flows into Lake St. John, and takes its rise in Lake Manouan. Pipmuakin River.

At the point where we entered it has a breadth of 200 yards. Proceeding up the river a distance of sixteen miles, course N. 20° W., a fall of fifty feet was reached. The stream below this flows with a slow current, varied by several short rapids, and passes through hills with from two to four hundred feet elevation, the whole having been burned over by frequent fires.

Manouan River

Beyond this fall the river narrows, becoming rapid, and continues so for eight miles, while the surrounding hills reach elevations from six to eight hundred feet above its level, and form a ridge extending from north-east to south-west. The river then flows with a slow uniform current for ten miles, course N 10° E. through a country covered by low rounded hills, lying apparently in ridges, having a north-and-south direction. Beyond this the river spreads out, becoming very rapid and shallow for a distance of three miles. Here we left it, and proceeded by a portage route for nineteen miles, course north, through several small lakes and brooks to avoid a long bend in the river full of rapids and impractible for canoe travel.

The river was again reached about one mile below Lake Manouan, and continuing up it we entered that lake October 3rd.

Lake Manouan.

On arriving at Lake Manouan we passed around the north side, making a time survey of the lake, which was completed on the 8th.

This is another very irregular lake, being about twenty-two miles long from east to west, with several large deep bays on either side running north and south. Over most of its area it is studded with many islands, both great and small. The country around the lake is almost flat, being broken by ridges of hills only to the south and west. These rise not more than 300 feet above the lake, but have the appearance of high mountains from their contrast with the general flatness of the surrounding country. About one-half of the timber is destroyed by fire; what remains consists of white and black spruce, balsam-spruce and white birch, few trees exceeding eight inches in diameter at three feet from the ground.

Peribonka River.

We awaited the arrival of Mr. Bignell on Lake Manouan until the 14th, when, fearing that we would be frozen in before reaching the Peribonka River, we started by a portage-route from the west side of Lake Manouan, and passed through several small lakes connected by a small brook flowing into a branch of the Peribonka about twelve miles from Lake Manouan. On reaching this branch we descended it about sixteen miles, reaching the main river one-half mile below Lake Onistagan; general course, south-west. This lake is several miles long by two miles broad. Crossing it on the 16th, we continued up the Peribonka River, and reached a stream from the west, which enters the river about two miles below the main forks, being distant thirty miles from Lake Onistagan; course, a few degrees east of north.

The Peribonka, for the first twenty miles, varies from two to three hundred yards in width, and has little current, but for the remainder of the distance is narrow and full of heavy rapids. The country along the river is similar to that described around Lake Manouan. The forests here have also been devastated by fire. What remains of them shows a larger growth of trees than the last mentioned.

We ascended the tributary from the west six miles to a small lake, which, being found partly frozen over, we were compelled to discontinue our canoe voyage on October 23rd. A permanent camp was formed, and Mr. Bignell joined us on November 4th, he having been stopped by ice on the Peribonka, about fifteen miles from Lake Onistagan. Winter camp.

After making toboggans for the transport of provisions and outfit, and as none of our party knew the route to Lake Mistassini, awaiting the arrival of a guide, we left the camp November 27th, and arrived at the Height of Land December 9th. The route travelled follows the branch, which flows through a chain of large lakes lying between ranges of low hills stretching from north to south. These hills have an average elevation of not more than fifty feet above the water-level. The land near the lakes, which cover the greater part of the surface of the country, is of a swampy character, clad with a thick growth of small black spruce and larch, and is wholly unfit for purposes of agriculture. The distance from the lake camp to the Height of Land is about forty miles, course nearly west. The lakes are well stocked with fish. Game is not abundant. Few ducks were seen on account of the absence of proper feeding-grounds, and no traces of moose or caribou were met with.

On crossing the Height of Land, we descended about 300 feet in twelve miles to Lake Temiscamie, a long lake running north and south, varying from one to three miles in width and very deep. An outpost from the Mistassini establishment was formerly located here by the Hudson Bay Company, but was abandoned some years back, as the Indians formerly trading here have either died or become accustomed to take their furs to Lake St. John for sale. Lake Temiscamie.

Following the Temiscamie River flowing out of the lake, which empties through Lake Mistassinis (Little Mistassini) into the great lake, for a distance of six miles, we passed through a very crooked lake about four miles long, and then continued down the river six miles, where we followed a portage route two miles long, and thus reached the north-east end of Lake Mistassinis on December 13th. The general course from Lake Temiscamie to this point is west-north-west. Lake Mistassinis.

The river continues almost parallel to the lake, and empties into it on the east side about thirty miles from its north end, running out again on the opposite side some distance farther north.

Lake Mistassinis, or Little Mistassini, is about fifty miles from north-east to south-west, lying parallel to the great lake, and is from one to eight miles wide, six miles being near the average breadth.

We passed down the east side to near the south-west end, where we crossed, and following a portage route through two small lakes about Lake Mistassini four miles long in all, thus reached Lake Mistassini at a point about thirty miles to the north-east of the Hudson Bay post. By passing down the east shore we arrived at the post on December 23rd, thus finishing a long and difficult tramp on snowshoes, having walked for the last ten days of the journey on very short rations, with the thermometer ranging to forty degrees below zero.

Shortly after our arrival I made arrangements with Mr. Miller, the gentleman in charge of the post, by which I obtained quarters in his house, and there set up the instruments and took regular meteorological observations during the month of January. At the end of this time, having had several disagreements with Mr. Bignell regarding the operations of the party, I determined to return to Ottawa, and having arranged with Mr. Miller to continue the meteorological observations during my absence, I left on the 2nd of February, accompanied by two men whom Mr. Bignell was sending to Lake St. John with letters. On leaving the post we proceeded to the south-west end of the lake, crossing the Height of Land near that point, and, after traversing several small lakes, reached a branch of the Chief River, followed it to its junction with the Chamouchouan River, and continued down the latter, reaching Lake St. John February 21st.

Two heavy snowstorms occurred while we were on the way, making the walking so difficult that our tent and sheet iron stove had to be abandoned, and we were obliged to sleep in the snow for more than a week.

The country passed through is very similar to that seen on the Peribonka River, and is described by Mr. W. McOuat in his report on the Mistassini River (Report of Progress Geol. Survey, 1871-72).

Since Mr. McOuat's exploration, the country has been wholly burned over, and few clumps of green woods remain.

Leaving Lake St. John February 23rd, I continued my journey with a horse and sleigh to Quebec, and reached Ottawa March 2nd. On the 23rd I received instructions to return to Mistassini, in charge of the party, and left Ottawa next day, accompanied by Mr. J. M. Macoun. Having been delayed in Montreal and Quebec, Lake St. John was not reached until April 5th.

Here we secured four men and provisions for the return trip through the kindness of Mr. J. H. Cummins, of the Hudson Bay Company, who also forwarded provisions for us to Lake Ashouapmouchouan, to be there stored until my men could return for them with canoes when the rivers had opened. Leaving Lake St. John, April 9th, with a party of eight, we started to return to Mistassini by the route taken by Mr. Jas. Richardson, a full report of which is given in the Geological Survey Report for 1870-71.

It was found necessary to travel mostly in the early morning, before the heat of the sun melted the crust on the snow. We therefore commenced our day's tramp about 3 a.m. and stopped about noon. We proceeded up the Chamouchouan River to the Shegobeesh Branch, and, following it to the lake at its head, crossed from it by a short portage to Lake Ashouapmouchouan, April 15th. Here, having replenished our stock of provisions, we continued up the Nikaubau River, through Lake Nikaubau and several smaller lakes, following the route laid down on Richardson's map, and reached the Height of Land. Mode of travelling.

Crossing this, we soon reached Lake Obatigoman, and, having passed along its eastern shore four miles, we passed overland to Lake Chibougamoo, arriving there on the 20th of April. Up to this time the weather, being cold and clear, was very favorable for travelling, but we were now overtaken by a period of mild weather, which made the snow so soft and heavy as to render tramping with loads almost impossible. In addition to this we were short of provisions, and on the 24th I decided to send four men ahead without loads, with instructions to reach the Hudson Bay post on Mistassini and send back provisions from there. These men travelled over sixty miles in forty hours, without food, and thus reached the post. From here two Indians were sent back with provisions to relieve us, and arrived at our camp, on the east side of Lake Chebougamoo, April 28th. Continuing our journey from this point, we reached the post next day. Delay.

On arriving at Mistassini I found Mr. Bignell encamped there, with about half his party, the remainder being engaged bringing in the canoes left on the Peribonka at the close of navigation. During my absence Mr. Bignell had returned to Lake Onistagan, and continued his survey from that point to the entrance of the Temiscamie River into Lake Mistassinis. Arrival at Mistassini

Mr. Bignell's party and my men were unable to move until May 28th, owing to the breaking up of the ice and the opening of navigation. Mr. Bignell, with his party, then descended to Lake St. John, while I sent six men, with three canoes, to Lake Ashouapmouchouan, to bring in the provisions drawn and stored there during the winter. After a very rough and dangerous trip, owing to the spring freshets in the rivers, the men returned on the 27th of June.

Mr. Macoun and myself were employed during their absence in keeping meteorological observations, determining the latitude of the post, and in collecting specimens of, and making notes on, the natural history of the vicinity. Having engaged two Indians as guides, we left the post June 30th, and, passing up the lake, reached the end of Mr. McOuat's survey on the west side, three miles beyond the discharge of the lake, on July 3rd.

Having determined the latitude of this point, we continued the survey to the north end, and thence back down the east side, connecting again with McOuat's survey at the "Big Narrows." The distances were measured with a Rochon micrometer, the angles with a transit theodolite, and frequent observations for latitude were made with the sextant as a check on the scaling.

Having completed the survey of the lake, we returned to the Hudson Bay post July 22nd. Being short of provisions, in consequence of one-half of our supply of pork having been stolen by Indians from the camp at Lake Ashouapmouchouan, I now determined to send my men back to Lake St. John.

Mr. Macoun and myself remained at the post until the arrival of the Hudson Bay Company's canoes from Rupert House, and had made arrangements to descend the Rupert River with them on their return trip to James Bay. This delayed us till the 22nd of August.

Lake Mistassini.

Père Charles Albanel.

The first person who has left any written account of his explorations of Lake Mistassini was Père Charles Albanel, a Jesuit missionary, who crossed it, in 1672, on his way from Lake St. John to Hudson Bay, which he reached by descending the Rupert River.

The following account of his exploration is taken from the "Relations des Jesuits dans la Nouvelle France," vol. iii, pp. 49-50, entitled "Voyage de la Mer du Nord par terre, et la découverte de la Baie de Hudson. Mission de Saint François-Xavier, en 1671 et 1672. Pere Chas. Albanel:"—

"Le 18 (June) nous entrasmes dans le grand Lac des Mistassirmins, qu'on tient estre si grande qu'il faut vingt jours de beau temps pour en faire le tour. Ce Lac tire son nom des rochers dont il est remply, qui sont d'une prodigieuse grosseur; il y a quantité de très belles iles du gibier, et du poissons de toute espece, les orignaux, les ours, les caribous, le porc-epic, et les castors y sont en abondance. Nous avions déja fait six lieuës au travers des iles qui l'entrecoupent, quand j'aperçeu comme une éminence de terre d'aussi loin que la veuë se peut estendre; je demanday à nos gens si c'estoit vers cet endroit qu'ils nous falloit aller? 'Tais-toy,' me dit nostre guide, 'ne le regarde point, si tu ne veux perir.'

"Les sauvages de toutes ces contrées s'imaginent que quiconque veut traverser ce lac se doit soigneusement garder de la curiosité de regarder cette route, et principalement le lieu où l'on doit aborder, son seul aspect, disent-ils cause l'agitation des eaux, et forme des tempestes qui font transir de frayeur les plus assurer."

The above is all that Père Albanel has written concerning the lake, and as he must have crossed only the southern end on his way to the Rupert River portage, he could speak only by hearsay of the remainder of the lake. He probably obtained his idea of the lake, and the number of days required to make the tour, from the Indians living around it, and if they were not more truthful than their present descendants now are, their testimony was not to be relied on. Six leagues is about the distance he would have had to travel down the south-east bay before reaching the islands off the point, at the present crossing place, and here the islands are about six miles distant from either shore. He could not have remained long at Mistassini, as he arrived at Lake Nemiskou, on the Rupert River, on June 25th, and six days are required to canoe that distance.

The next explorer to reach Mistassini was the French botanist Michaux, who, in 1792, ascended the Mistassini River from Lake St. John, and traversed the lake to the Rupert River, intending to descend it to James Bay, but, owing to the season being far advanced, he abandoned this project and returned to Lake St. John. Michaux followed the route taken by Père Albanel, and quotes him for his description. Michaux.

The Hudson Bay Company have had a trading post on the shores of the lake for over one hundred years. This post was first situated near the outlet, but owing to the difficulty in procuring an adequate supply of fish, the staple article of food, the post was removed, over fifty years ago, to its present position on the south-east bay. During the time of the North-West Trading Company, they also had a trading post at the southern end of the south-east bay.

In 1870, Mr. Jas. Richardson, of the Geological Survey, was sent to explore the country to the north of Lake St. John. He ascended the Chamouchouan River, and reached the southern end of Mistassini, but, owing to the failure of his supply of provisions, he was obliged to return without seeing the main body of the lake. Geological Survey.

The next year, Mr. Walter McOuat was sent out to continue the survey. He proceeded from Lake St. John by the Mistassini River, making a survey of the route followed, and succeeded in surveying about one-half of the shore line of the lake, when he also was obliged to return for want of provisions.

Nothing farther was done towards finishing the survey until, owing to the request of the Quebec Geographical Society in 1883, the present expedition was dispatched by the Geological Survey and the Quebec Government. As the season was far advanced before the party was formed, it was deemed advisable to delay its departure until the season of 1884.

Derivation. The name Mistassini is formed from two Algonkin words—"mista," signifying big, and "assine," a stone; and is so called because of the large boulders of gneiss strewn along the west shore.

Size. Lake Mistassini is a long and narrow body of water, stretching from north-east to south-west, with a perceptible curve between the ends, the concavity of the curve being towards the south-east. It lies between N. Lat. 50° and 51° 24', W. Long. 72° 45' to 74° 20'. The length, in a straight line between the extremities of the north-east and south-west bays, is nearly one hundred miles, the average breadth of the main body being about twelve miles. At either end of the lake, a long point stretches out, dividing the ends into two deep bays. Between the points, and seemingly a continuation of them, is a long chain of rocky islands, which, by overlapping each other, almost divide the lake into two parts, so that a view of the opposite side is rarely obtained in going around the shore. A slight decrease in the present level of the lake would result in the production of two separate lakes, as the water between the islands is quite shallow, and forms a contrast in this respect with the great depth between the islands and shore on either side. Here the lake is very deep, an isolated sounding, made in crossing, having given 374 feet at a point which, I was informed, was not the deepest part of the lake.

The bay at the south-east end of the lake is called Abatagush. This bay, sixteen miles from its mouth, is again divided by a long point into two other bays. About four miles from the end of this point, and on it, the Hudson Bay post is situated.

Cabistachuan Bay. The eastern part, called Cabistachuan Bay, runs slightly east of south, in an irregular course, for about twelve miles, the Little Perch River coming in at its head. The western part is much larger and more irregular. It stretches south for sixteen miles, a small river from Lake Wakiniche falling into it at that distance. A side branch of the bay runs to the westward for upwards of ten miles. The general width of Abatagush Bay is one and one-half miles. The south-west, or Poonichaun Bay, for a distance of twenty miles from its entrance, has an average breadth of about five miles. Its shores are broken by smaller bays, and its surface is covered with islands, varying from six miles long, by one and one-half wide, to mere boulders. After the first twenty miles, the bay narrows to an average breadth of less than one-half mile, and continues in a south-westerly course for a long distance, as the end was not reached after ascending it fourteen miles. The Indians say that a large river empties into the lake at the head of this bay. The north-east and north-west bays are not so deep as the southern ones; the distance from the end of the point to the mouth of the Northern rivers. Papasqutsatee River, a large stream coming in at the head of the north-west bay, being fifteen miles, with an average breadth of rather more than four miles. From the mouth of the Toquaoco River, which enters the north-east bay at its head, to the end of the point, the distance is nineteen miles, the average breadth being under four miles. By this river a canoe route goes to a Hudson Bay post, called Nitchicoon, situated on a branch of the East Main River, to the north-east. This stream falls rapidly during the dry season, being an exception to the other rivers running into the lake, which, taking their rise in large lakes, are not greatly affected by local rainfall.

Beside those above referred to, the large river flowing out of Lake Temiscamie, and passing through Lake Mistassini, enters the lake on the east side about twenty miles from the head of the north-east bay. Almost directly opposite this river, on the west side, a smaller stream, called the Wabassinon River, enters.

The shore of the lake is indented by a number of smaller bays, and many islands also occur along its margin.

The shores of the lake are mostly rocky, with no marshes or beach, a fact accounting for the absence of any great numbers of wading birds or graminaceous ducks. The western bank rises from thirty to sixty feet above the surface of the water, and is in many places perpendicular. The eastern bank is not so elevated, and rises more gradually.

To the south of Mistassini, and running north of east, is a ridge of hills forming an escarpment about 300 feet high, and constituting the Height of Land between the waters flowing to the St. Lawrence and those draining to Hudson Bay, and the division line between the Province of Quebec and the North-east Territory. To the north is another range, passing within ten miles of the lake and trending away to the westward. The highest of these hills does not rise more than 500 feet above the level of the lake. Hills.

The country in the vicinity of the lake is generally slightly rolling, with rounded hills, rising from thirty to sixty feet above the water, and interspersed with numerous small lakes and marshes.

As will be seen from the following summary, compiled from the daily meterological observations taken at the Hudson Bay post on Mistassini, which are given in detail in Appendix (II), the climate unfits the surrounding country for purposes of agriculture, as frosts occur during every month except July.

I am told that the season of 1885 was a good average of the climate here, except that the rainfall was excessive.

SUMMARY OF METEOROLOGICAL OBSERVATIONS, LAKE MISTASSINI, 1885.

	Jan.	Feb.	March.	April.	May.	June.	July.	August.
Mean temperature ...	−18.5	−10.7	01.9	25.3	42.3	53.1	50.9	56.7
Highest temperature	16	39	35	54	85	79	76	81
Lowest temperature.	−56	−46	−47	−10	08	30	39	31
Monthly range	72	85	82	73	77	49	37	50
Mean maximum temperature	−05.1	11.1	16.6	30.6	53.0	64.7	67.0	68.1
Mean minimum temperature	−31.6	−10.2	−18.0	16.0	29.3	39.4	49.8	45.7
Mean daily range ...	26.5	20.3	34.6	14.6	24.3	25.3	17.2	22.4
Number of days' rain				4	17	20		21
Number of days' snow	13	10	13	8	2	2	....	
Number of fair days ...	12	16	19	16	12	12	....	9
Resultant direction of wind ..	N.45°E.	N.56°E.	N.74°E.	N.20°E.	N.48°W	S.80°W	S.40°W	S.67 W

Snow covers the ground about the middle of October, and remains until late in May, all the smaller lakes being frozen over during that time.

The main body of Lake Mistassini is an exception, as owing to its depth and consequent slow change of temperature, it does not generally freeze over before December 20th, and opens a couple of weeks later than the other lakes in spring.

During the summer months the sky is clouded a greater part of the time, accompanied by drizzing rains and heavy thunder storms. The soil of the country overlying the limestone basin, on and about Lake Mistassini, is a sandy loam with clay subsoil, and would yield good crops in a more favorable climate.

Short summer.

On the main body of the lake, and to the northward, the summer season is shorter and colder than in the vicinity of the post. During the month of July, the low lands bordering the lake were frozen solid within one foot of the surface, in all places where the trees were at all dense. This marked difference is undoubtedly due to the proximity to such a large body of cold water, which lowers the general temperature of the air during the warmer portions of the year. The soil overlying the Laurentian gneisses and schists is light and sandy, only a thin layer generally resting on these rocks.

Agriculture.

At the Hudson Bay post, the most favorable point on the lake for agriculture, a poor crop of potatoes is raised yearly. They are small, as the tops are always frozen before reaching maturity. In the spring, as soon as the frost was out of the ground, I sowed garden peas, beans, corn, and turnips. On August 20th the peas were beginning to fill the pods, the beans were in flower, and the corn only eighteen inches above the ground; the turnips alone were growing nicely. I believe that barley has been sown here, but would not ripen. A full list of trees and plants, with their distribution, is given in Appendix (I) by Mr. Macoun, and I will only add that no timber of commercial value was seen near the lake.

Covering the higher ground, at the southern end, white spruce, poplar, balsam-spruce and white birch trees were found, some of which had a diameter of eighteen inches, three feet from the ground. The swamps are covered with a thick growth of small-sized black spruce and tamarac, and the small areas of burned land are generally clad with a second-growth of banksian pine. Trees.

Mr. Macoun, in his report, also gives a list of the birds found about the lake. The waters of Mistassini and all the adjoining large lakes are full of fish. The principal kinds are lake-trout, river-trout, whitefish, pike, pickerel, and sucker, all of large size and fine quality. These fisheries would be of considerable commercial value if access could be had to them by railway. Fish.

Fish is the chief article of food of the Indians around the lake. During the spawning season in the autumn, when the fish come into the shallow water, large numbers are caught in nets, then cleaned and smoked for the winter supply. In the winter, the fish are caught on hooks through holes in the ice. The Hudson Bay Company's people also catch and salt a large quantity.

There are twenty-six families of Indians, about one hundred and twenty-five persons in all, living around the lake and trading with the Hudson Bay Company there. These Indians speak a dialect of the Algonkin language, and belong to the Mistassini tribe of that great family. They are mostly short, and of poor physique, although there are exceptions to the rule. Very few of them are now of pure Indian blood. They live by hunting fur-bearing animals during the winter, the skins of which they barter with the Hudson Bay Company for flour and other provisions, and articles of clothing. Indians.

As there are no longer any deer in the country, and small game, such as rabbits and partridges, are scarce; if it were not for the provisions supplied by the Company, these Indians would be unable to live. As it is, cases of death by starvation are by no means uncommon during the winter. In the summer, all the able-bodied men descend the Rupert River in large canoes to Rupert House, with the furs taken during the winter, and return with supplies for the ensuing year.

The greater part of these Indians can read and write in the Cree characters, and have several books printed in that form. They all profess Christianity, although it is mingled with their old beliefs, as they still have their sorcerers, who profess to be able to do many things by the aid of evil spirits. A missionary, under the Church Missionary Society of England, comes inland from Hudson Bay once in two or three years, and performs the ceremonies of marriage and christening as required. During his absence, one of the Indians conducts the church service at all gatherings.

GENERAL DESCRIPTION OF THE RUPERT RIVER.

As the journey from Lake Mistassini to Rupert House was hurried, and consequently large areas of country were passed over in a short space of time, I will, in the following, give extracts from my daily journal *en route* :—

August 22nd.—Mr. Macoun and myself left the Hudson Bay post at Mistassini at 4 p.m., in a large canoe, with ten men paddling, and camped for the night at the "Big Narrows," eighteen miles from the post.

August 23rd.—Started at daybreak, and crossed the lake to the west side; proceeded up the shore to the Portage Bay, distant ten miles from the outlet of the river. Here, passing over a low, rocky ridge, by a portage two hundred yards long, we entered the Rupert River, and descended it a distance of ten miles, in a course of N. 16° W., to a short portage, crossing a long point, made to avoid heavy rapids in the river. Camped on the portage.

Rupert River.

The outlet of Lake Mistassini is about one hundred yards wide. Immediately below this the river spreads out, and forms numerous channels between the islands with which it is covered. The river is so covered, and has a breadth varying from one-quarter to two miles, as far as the last portage. The surrounding country is almost flat, with low, rounded hills, never exceeding fifty feet elevation above the level of the river. The timber is principally black spruce and white birch, with poplar, tamarac and banksian pine: all of small size, never having a diameter exceeding six inches, three feet from the ground. Timber burnt near the portages.

August 24th.—Continued down the river, now narrowing to a breadth varying from one hundred yards to one mile, having a swift current, with several small rapids which are passed by portages in ascending the river. The river continues full of small rocky islands. Distance travelled to-day thirty miles in a general northerly course. The country passed is not so flat as yesterday, some hills rising from seventy-five to one hundred feet above the river. The prevailing timber is black spruce, birch, banksian pine and tamarac, all of small size.

The greater part of the south-west side has been burnt, and is covered with a second-growth of white birch. The north-east shore is unburnt, and black spruce predominates.

Heavy gale from the west, with showers of rain, all day, making it very cold and disagreeable to travel.

25th. Continued down the river eleven miles to Lake Miskittenow, through the east end of which the river flows.

This lake is seven miles long, course west, with an average breadth of one and one-half miles. On the north side of the west end is a hill of about three hundred feet elevation, forming a conspicuous landmark and called Miskittenow Mountain. Leave the Rupert.

Leaving the river, we passed to the upper end of the lake, and thence, by a portage of 1,100 yards, to Lake Kanataikow. Passing through this lake, which is very crooked, for nine miles, we crossed a portage, one-quarter mile long, to a small lake called Kakomenhane, and then through it three miles to the portage at the opposite end, where camp was made for the night. General course of travel for the day, N. 55° W. The country passed through was rougher than yesterday, with rounded hills rising from one to three hundred feet above the general level.

The timber consists of small spruce, birch, banksian pine and tamarac, mostly of second-growth.

26th.—Left camp at daybreak, and, crossing the portage, 250 yards long, entered Wabistan Lake, the head of the Marten branch of the Rupert River. We followed this lake eight miles to its outlet by a small brook 300 yards long, then across a small lake one and a-quarter miles, and down the river two and a-quarter miles, to another small lake, and on through Lake Mok-how-as-took for thirteen miles. Thence through seven small lakes connected by the river. Total distance, forty-seven miles; direction, N. 60° W. Timber very small and mostly of second-growth banksian pine, with black spruce and birch. Marten branch.

27th.—Continued down the Marten River, passing three small lakes in thirteen miles to Jacob's Lake, and through it eleven miles. Its shores are burnt and covered with large boulders. From here down the river ten miles to Robert's Lake, camping at its outlet, five miles from the inlet. Total distance, forty miles; course, N. W. The country was flatter than yesterday, no hills exceeding one hundred and fifty feet in elevation. Much more burnt land was seen than on previous days. The timber was very small, no trees exceeding six inches in diameter, three feet from the ground, and consisted principally of black spruce. A few small balsam-spruce were seen on the low river bank during the afternoon.

28th.—Heavy frost last night. Travelled all day on the Marten River, passing through four lakes, called, respectively, Ka-wo-wat-in-ou, Te-say-kow, Cooper's and Gull; also made portages past several small rapids in the river. Total distance, thirty-six miles; direction, N. W. Country flatter than yesterday, and densely wooded with black spruce and tamarac, with little birch. Not much burnt land. Soil poor and swampy or bare rock. Lakes.

29th.—Continued down the Marten River, passing five small chutes by portages, the aggregate fall in seventeen miles being one hundred and ten feet.

Re-enter Rupert River

Here the Marten enters the Rupert River. Passing down the Rupert, which here has an average breadth of one-half mile, the Nitchicoon branch was passed, two and a-half miles below.

By this river the canoes bound for the Hudson Bay post at Nitchicoon, on the East Main River, leave the Rupert, and reach that river through a system of lakes similar to that passed on the Marten.

Continuing down the Rupert, with a swift current, for six miles, a fall and rapid of twenty feet is passed by a portage one-half mile long; thence the river runs with a swift current three miles, to the entrance

Lake Nemiscow

of Lake Nemiskow. Passing down the lake eight miles, we camped on a small island, where the Hudson Bay Company have stored a supply of provisions for the Indians wintering in the vicinity. The country passed through to-day was much lower than yesterday, being nearly flat; the timber much the same, with more second-growth birch and poplar of small size. Lake Nemiskow is silted up by the detritus brought down by the river for a distance of two miles beyond where we camped, and is characterized by low islands and sand-banks, clad with willow-bush and reeds, through which a channel, half a mile wide, runs.

30th.—Proceeded down the lake to an encampment of Indians from Rupert House, who were engaged netting and smoking small sturgeon for winter use. Left again at 2.30 p.m., and followed the north-east bay six and a-half miles to the smaller discharge.

Lake Nemiskow is made up of three deep bays, forming a Y; each being about fifteen miles long, with an average breadth of three miles. The Rupert River flows in by the south-east bay, and out again about half-way up the north-east, having two outlets, the larger being several miles farther north than the smaller. A large river flows into the south-west bay, and forms the canoe route to Washwanaby, a Hudson Bay post on the Notaway River. Several other large streams flow into the lake.

The surrounding country is comparatively flat, being highest to the south-west, where the hills probably have an elevation above the water of 200 feet. To the north and east is much lower and swampy. The waters of the lake are shallow.

Père Albanel says, in the Relations des Jesuits, that ten days are required to make a circuit of the lake, and that it is surrounded by high mountains, forming a semicircle from south to north.

Leaving by the smaller discharge, we descended it two miles to a portage 600 yards long, past a rapid and fall of forty feet. Camped at the end of portage. The timber was slightly better than yesterday, with bluffs of poplar and birch along the lake, and no burnt land.

31st.—Continuing down stream, the main discharge was reached by a portage one-quarter mile long, past a rapid with ten feet of fall, distant four and one-half miles from camp; the general course from Lake Nemiskow to this point being N. 20° W. The river now runs with a swift current, and small rapids, twenty-six miles in a course N. 50° W. to the Oatmeal Fall. This, like the other falls on the river, consists of a chute, with heavy rapids at the bottom. Oatmeal Fall.

The Oatmeal Fall is passed by a portage one and a-quarter miles long. Below it, at a distance of two and three-quarter miles, another fall, thirty-five feet high, called the White Beaver, entails a further portage of half-a-mile. Beyond this, the river flows rapidly for seven and a-half miles to where we camped for the night.

The country passed was very flat until the Oatmeal Fall was reached, below which the river flows in a valley, between banks from thirty to fifty feet high. Above this no distinct valley was observed. The timber becomes larger and better as we descend, and no burnt woods were seen, except on the portages and between the Oatmeal and White Beaver Falls.

September 1st.—Proceeding down the river, between banks from twenty to fifty feet high, for six miles, the first portage of "The Fours" was reached. This portage, three-quarters of a mile long, passes a heavy rapid and fall of fifty feet. One-half mile below is the second portage, over a chute of seventy-five feet; then, three-quarters of a mile to the third chute of fifty feet, passed by a portage of half-a-mile and down heavy rapids to the last portage, over rapids with a fall of thirty feet in quarter of a mile.

The country was higher to-day and the soil better. The timber was much larger. Balsam-poplar was first seen since leaving Mistassini, also balsam-spruce, with the exception of a few trees on the Marten river mentioned above. White spruce, having a diameter of twenty inches, three feet from the ground, was observed on the portages at "The Fours." Very little of the timber is burnt. The country seems to be descending in a series of low terraces, similar to those seen on the shores of the St. Lawrence River; each fall on the Rupert being caused by the passage of the river over an escarpment. Timber.

September 2nd.—For seven miles the river flows with a moderate current, with one small rapid, three-quarters of a mile long, to the Shekash portage, one and a-quarter miles long, passing a rapid and chute of seventy-five feet. Beyond this, the moderate current continues for ten miles, when another chute of twenty feet is passed by the Cat portage, one-quarter mile long. The river then again flows steadily for eleven miles, to another rapid of twenty feet, where we camped. As far as the Cat portage, the river flows between clay banks from twenty to forty feet high, densely wooded with large poplar and white spruce, below this, the country became very flat and swampy, covered with small black spruce, tamarac and second-growth poplar. General course travelled during the day, N. 70° W.

3rd.—Started early to-day, running the Plum-pudding rapid, one and a-half miles long, with fifteen feet fall, and thence two miles to Smoke Hill rapid, having a fall of twenty-five feet, and passed by a portage of one mile. Below, the river runs with a moderate current for ten miles, when the last rapid, one mile long, with ten feet fall, full of large boulders, was run, and Rupert House, one mile below, was reached.

Rupert House.

Rupert House is situated at the mouth of the river, which empties into Rupert Bay, an extension of James Bay.

At this point the river has a width of upwards of one mile, and discharges a volume of water estimated equal to that of the Ottawa River at Ottawa.

The country between Plum-Pudding Rapid and the mouth of the river is very flat and swampy, covered with only a fair growth of timber. The soil is chiefly a heavy clay, and is generally too wet and cold for agricultural purposes.

Return to Ottawa.

At Rupert House, garden vegetables are cultivated with fair success: barley is also grown, but seldom ripens, owing to the shortness of the season and frosts during the summer. At Rupert House our season's work was completed, and we hastened to return to Ottawa. We were not able to leave, however, until the 9th, when we crossed the foot of James Bay to Moose Factory, a distance of one hundred and twenty miles, in a large canoe, with six men. The water of the bay is very shallow; so much so, that when the tide is out, nothing but mud flats can be seen.

Having been delayed by high winds, Moose Factory was not reached until the 14th. Having here changed our canoe for a smaller one, with three men, we started up the Moose River next day, and reached Dog Lake, at the Height of Land, on the 29th. Here taking the Canadian Pacific Railway, we arrived in Ottawa October 2nd.

Geological Notes.

With the exception of the comparatively small areas of Huronian and Cambrian rocks, found in the vicinity of Lake Mistassini, the Laurentian gneisses and associated rocks occupy the whole country from the Gulf of St. Lawrence to James Bay, along the route traversed by this expedition. Of these rocks, the red gneiss, composed of red orthoclase, grey quartz and black mica, predominates; with hornblende gneisses and schists, mica schists, crystalline limestones, and an area of triclinic feldspar rocks.

In the following pages a detailed statement of the rocks met with in ascending the Betsiamites River and on the route to Lake Mistassini and James Bay is given.

The rocks are first seen on the Betsiamites, seven miles from its mouth, and opposite the mouth of the Nepee River, where the hills of the Laurentian range are entered. Between this point and the coast, the river flows between sand-banks, with an elevation varying from twenty to fifty feet.

The first hundred feet of the exposure is dark-red, coarse-grained gneiss, composed of red orthoclase, grey quartz and mica. Dip S. 50° W. at a high angle. Then, for 600 feet, light red, fine-grained gneiss, in which the quartz greatly predominates, banded with coarse dark-red gneiss, composed chiefly of red orthoclase and grey quartz, with a small quantity of dark-green decomposed hornblende and mica. Also light-greyish gneiss, containing large proportions of black mica and dark-green hornblende. One hundred yards beyond the last, dark-red, coarse-grained gneiss, alternating with fine-grained bands for fifty yards. Exposures of gneiss.

Two and a-half miles farther up the river, an exposure of seventy-five feet was seen, the rocks being fine-grained red gneiss, alternating with bands of dark-grey hornblende and mica-schist.

One mile beyond was seen coarse-grained red gneiss, containing large crystals of pink orthoclase and black mica, with dark-grey quartz, for one hundred yards.

The next exposure occurred two miles further up the river, and consisted of fine-grained dark-grey gneiss, composed of light-grey orthoclase, black mica and a small quantity of quartz. Dip S. 60° E. $<60°$.

Then, two miles to coarse-grained red gneiss, some of which exhibits no signs of bedding, and resembles the granite. The length of this exposure is about two hundred yards. Two miles beyond is fine-grained grey and red gneiss, the former predominating. Dip N. 60° W. < 50.

No outcrops now occur on the river for twenty-one miles, when the following fine exposure was seen. The section, in ascending order, is as follows:—Thirty feet, dark-grey gneiss, containing masses of almost pure pink orthoclase; then thirty feet of coarse red gneiss, composed chiefly of red orthoclase and grey quartz, resembling graphic granite. Many dark-red garnets, as large as peas, are scattered through this rock in bands. Above this is twenty-five feet of fine-grained grey gneiss, highly micaceous, and then twenty feet of highly quartziferous gneiss, containing quantities of large orthoclase crystals and a little mica. Above this, fifty feet of alternate bands of red and grey gneiss, varying in color with the quantity of mica present, and from the same cause changing in texture being fine-grained when an excess of that mineral is present. The dip of these bands is S. 40° E. < 60°.

The next exposure occurs about four miles beyond the last and two miles below the first fall. The rocks consist of red and grey gneiss. Similar exposures, having a dip N. 60° W. < 45 – 60°, are seen at the falls. On the shore, immediately below the fall, are large beds of iron and garnet sands. These have been washed there by the strong eddy in river at this point, having been carried down from some point farther up the stream, where they are formed by the disintegration of the iron-bearing gneisses subsequently mentioned. Red and grey gneisses were seen, at distances of one, two, four and nine miles above the falls, having a dip of S. 60° E. < 70°.

At the foot of the four-mile portage, and fourteen miles above the first fall, was seen a yellowish-grey gneiss, composed chiefly of quartz and mica, and covered with a film of black oxide of iron about one-eighth of an inch thick. This rock is a decomposition product of the ordinary red gneiss, charged with grains of magnetic iron, and has been formed in the manner described in a subsequent paragraph. A short distance beyond, these rocks were found highly charged with magnetite in small grains. Dip N. 20° W. < 75°. Six miles beyond, greyish and pink gneiss, apparently holding much iron outcrops, with a strike S. 70° W. Three miles farther, dark red coarse-grained gneiss strike S. 50° W.

Iron.

At a small fall, three and a-half miles above the last exposure, is a red gneiss, weathering a pale buff, and highly charged with magnetic iron in lenticular beds and small grains. The beds vary in width along their course from half an inch to eight inches.

At the second small lake on the ten-mile portage, an exposure of coarse-grained red granitoid gneiss was seen. On the fourth lake occurs fine banded red gneiss. Dip S. 45° E. < 45°. Interstratified with these are beds of a micaceous iron ore, seemingly of great extent. These beds are not pure, but in the form of a gneiss, composed of quartz, mica and hornblende, with a very large percentage of iron ore.

On the last lake of the portage, besides the red gneiss, loose angular blocks of a dark greyish-blue trap, containing minute crystals of dark green hornblende and grains of dark grey quartz, were seen scattered along the shore, and had evidently not travelled far. Considerable beds of the iron-bearing rocks are also seen on the lake, interstratified with the red gneiss.

Trap.

The next exposure occurs on the river at the end of the ten-mile portage, and consists of buff and red gneisses. These buff rocks are a decomposition-product of the red, the feldspar being dissolved out, leaving a friable sandstone, consisting of quartz and magnetic grains, these being probably the source of the beds of iron-sands found along the river and coast.

Similar exposures were seen at intervals along the shores of Lake Natuakimin.

Three miles up the river beyond this lake, and fifty-eight miles from the first fall, occurs an outcrop of pink crystalline limestone, coarsely granular in structure, and containing crystals of mica and sphene.

A short distance beyond is a dark grey stratified dioritic rock, composed chiefly of quartz hornblende and triclinic feldspar, and just beyond pink crystalline limestone again occurs, and here holds crystals of a bluish-grey plageoclase.

No exposures now occur on the river for thirteen miles, to where the stream turns eastward and breaks through the Labradorite hills for six miles to Lake Pipmuakin. The first rock here seen was a bluish- Labradorite grey massive plageoclase feldspar, containing large crystals of the same mineral. This is followed by a dark bluish-black feldspar rock, with hornblende. Half a mile beyond, a gneiss, made up of plageoclase quartz and mica, occurs, and is followed by coarse-grained dark plageoclase rock, weathering grey, and containing grains of magnetic iron ore.

One mile from Lake Pipmuakin was seen a dark grey triclinic feldspar rock, weathering to a light yellow. Dip S. 70° E. <70°. At this point a conspicuous fault occurs on the south side of the river; the hill is broken through its centre, and the east side has subsided fully thirty feet.

The above rocks are probably part of the area of plageoclase rock traced by Mr. F. Adams to the north and east of Lake St. John. They continue about three miles along the north-west shore of Lake Pipmuakin, where they give place to a coarse-grained red gneiss, and just beyond a dark grey orthoclase gneiss. The contact between the plageoclase rocks and the orthoclase gneisses was not seen, being covered with drift.

One mile beyond the last exposure is a light grey quartzite, containing considerable quantities of black mica, with a strike of N. 10° W. This is followed in two miles by dark grey fine-grained gneiss, composed chiefly of quartz and black hornblende, with orthoclase. Dip N. 40° E. <75°. At the entrance of the north-west bay was seen red and grey gneiss, changing in colour with the different proportions of quartz, hornblende and orthoclase. Similar exposures occur on the small islands in the bay and at the mouth of the Pipmuakin River.

Probable Huronian Conglomerate. Many boulders of a conglomerate were seen strewn along the shore of the lake, having a matrix of crystalline limestone, holding gneiss pebbles. No rock exposures were observed along the Pipmuakin River, although near the point where the portage route leaves it for the Manouan River, loose angular blocks of a white crystalline limestone are scattered over the surface, and evidently not much travelled.

On the third and fourth lakes of the Manouan portage, the ordinary red and grey gneisses, composed of quartz, hornblende and orthoclase, were seen, having a dip S. 60° W. < 70°.

The next exposure occurs on the Manouan River, a short distance above the point where we entered it. The rock here seen was a dark green hornblendic gneiss, holding considerable quantities of magnetic iron. Dip S. 60° E. < 70°. Exposures of similar gneiss occur along the river as far as the portage to Lake Manouan. In these the darker varieties, containing large proportions of hornblende, predominate, and the greater number show signs of magnetite present.

On the fifth lake of the Lake Manouan portage route, a greyish-green crystalline limestone, containing large crystals of mica and hornblende, was found interstratified with the red gneiss. Some of the mica crystals found on the surface were six by four inches in diameter, and quite fit for purposes of commerce. The limestones were seen at intervals along the route for a distance of three miles. Beyond this, no exposures occur until Lake Manouan is reached.

Mica.

On the north side of the lake, three exposures of dark grey hornblendic gneiss were seen, having a dip N. 10° E. < 60°. At the first lake on the portage route from Lake Manouan to the Peribonka River, an outcrop of red fine-grained gneiss occurs. Dip S. 30° W. < 40°.

Nothing further was seen until the inlet of Lake Onistagan, on the Peribonka River, was reached, the rock here being dark grey hornblende-gneiss. Fifteen miles farther up the river is coarse-grained red and grey gneiss, containing a large proportion of quartz. Strike N. 30° W. At each of the small rapids beyond this point, light grey gneiss, composed chiefly of quartz and hornblende, with small quantities of orthoclase, was seen.

From the Peribonka River to Lake Mistassini, but few exposures were observed, as the country at the time we traversed it was covered with snow, which probably hid some of the few outcrops occurring.

The last exposure of gneiss was seen at the Crooked Lake, on the Temiscamie River, beyond the Height of Land; the next exposure being Cambrian limestone, on Lake Mistassinis, so that the junction of the two formations lies between these points.

To the westward, on the Ashouapmouchouan and Mistassini Rivers, similar Larentian rocks extend all the way from Lake St. John to the

Height of Land, and are described in the Reports of the Geological Survey 1870-71 and 1871-72, by Messrs. Richardson and McOuat. respectively.

From these observations it may be concluded that, with the exception of the comparative y small areas of Cambro-Silurian rocks in the neighborhood of Lake St. John, and perhaps similar small areas at other points not yet explored, all the rocks between the Gulf of St. Lawrence and the Height of Land are of Laurentian age. And these rocks probably extend far beyond to the shores of Hudson Straits, occupying the greater part of the Labrador peninsula, with but few areas of newer rock overlying. On the west side of Lake Mistassini, the coarse grained red gneiss, composed of quartz, orthoclase, mica and hornblende, appear with a general strike of N. 30° E. The space between Crooked Lake and this side being overlaid by the Cambrian limestones which extend to the western shore of the lake. On the Rupert River, the coarse-grained red gneiss predominates over the finer-grained varieties. Extent of Laurentian rocks.

At the junction of the Marten and Rupert Rivers, and for some distance below, a darker gneiss, containing larger quantities of dark green hornblende, appears. In the river, at the first portage of "The Fours," a dyke of dark greyish-green dioritic trap, over twenty yards wide, running S. 70° W., penetrates the red gneiss and holds gneissic fragments near the plane of junction. Trap dyke.

Farther down the river, the exposures are fewer; the last is at the House Rapid, one mile above Rupert House and consists of the common red gneiss. Strike W. 10° S.

HURONIAN.

A series of rocks similar to the epidotic and chloritic slates of the Shickshock Mountains and the Eastern Townships, is seen first about forty miles south-west of the southern extremity of Lake Mistassini. These rocks have been fully described by Mr. Richardson in the Geological Survey Report for 1870-71, from which the following is an extract:— Richardson's report.

"This series was first observed at the north end of Lake Abatagomaw. Thence it occupies the country along the line examined, to and along Lake Wakinitche, including Lake Chibogomou and the lakes and portages between it and Abatagomaw [large lakes lying south-west of Mistassini]. The last of it was seen at about two miles beyond the outlet of Lake Wakinitche, nearly four miles in a straight line from where it was first observed on Lake Abatagomaw. As already stated, the rocks of this series are met with almost immediately succeeding the Laurentian, near the north end of Lake Abatagomaw. Beyond this, they are well seen in a narrow bay running for several miles in a direction nearly east, where they occur both on the shore of the bay and on islands. The rocks here are green chloritic slates. In some places they contain crystals of hornblende, and are occasionally interstratified with dolomitic beds, weathering brown. The dip along this stretch is from N. 31° W. to N. 3° E. < 44° to 68°. On the first portage beyond this bay there are considerable exposures of flattened spheroidal or reniform masses, from a few inches to upwards of a foot in diameter. They are made up of an indurated greenish and purplish argillaceous rock, which is jaspery in its texture. When sections of these spheroids have been exposed to the weather, they present a concentric arrangement of various shades of color, becoming lighter towards the centre. The strike of these rocks is N. 61° E. and S. 61° W. To the end of the second portage, the rock is a greenish chloritic slate, becoming, in places, epidotic and dioritic, the latter variety assuming a reniform structure, and holding, between the concentric layers a soft dark greenish mineral, resembling serpentine. The next exposure is a little beyond the entrance of Lake Chibogomou, and is the only one met with for about four miles, on the main west shore, or on the islands immediately to the eastward. It is a quartzose feldspathic rock, with films of a greenish chloritic mineral. The feldspar is yellowish and the quartz greenish in hue. On an island about seven miles from the entrance to the lake, the rock is very similar, except that the chloritic mineral above mentioned occurs only in spots. Between the last two exposures, but somewhat to the eastward of them, there are two islands, composed of a yellowish micaceous granite. For the next four miles, as far as observed, on the north-east side of the lake and the islands adjacent, the rocks are a light grey and yellowish felsite, with quartz and minute scales of mica or talc. In some places these are associated with a green dioritic rock, in small bands, of from one to four feet wide, the strike of which is S. 33° E. and N. 33° W. If this banding is due to bedding, which is doubtful, it is the only indication of lines of stratification observed thus far on the lake.

"The next point at which the rock is seen on the same side is just before reaching Paint Mountain. Here it is a green chloritic rock, weathering to greyish green, and holding considerable quantities of magnetic iron ore disseminated in grains and crystals. Still closer to Paint Mountain, on the shore, the rocks are green chloritic slate, with no well-defined bedding. Here the yellow sulphuret of copper, which is described farther on, occurs. These rocks are also more or less charged with fine-grained iron pyrites, for a distance of about

Magnetic iron

Copper

a mile, to a point immediately below Paint Mountain, which rises above the lake, in a short distance back, to a height of 250 feet. In one place, there is a depression running up the mountain from the lake, thirty feet wide, filled with drift. The strike of this depression is S. 61° W. and N. 61° E. On Sorcerer's Mountain, which rises, on the south-east, to a height of 425 feet above the lake, the rock is green chloritic slate, with small specks of iron pyrites disseminated irregularly through it. In the narrows of the north-east end of the lake, the rock is a conglomerate and breccia. In some parts, it is made up of small fragments of the rocks already described; consisting of yellowish feldspar and quartz, green chlorite, serpentine, and epidote; while in others, the pieces are from a few ounces to one hundred pounds in weight. Large expanses of conglomerate are likewise entirely com- Conglomerate. posed of rounded fragments of Laurentian gneiss of grey and red colors, the latter predominating. Other exposures show a conglomerate made up of angular and rounded fragments from an ounce to a ton weight, in a matrix of fine material of the same kind. These conglomerates are succeeded by serpentines and associated rocks, which make their appearance immediately to the west of the first portage leading from the lake. About 200 yards west of the portage-road, a cone-shaped hill, which rises over the waters of the narrows about one hundred and sixty feet, is entirely composed of serpentine. This rock is traced, on one side, to the portage, and on the other it is supposed to form part of Juggler's Mountain, which is about 400 feet high, and is about two miles distant, bearing S. 41° W. On the highest part of the cone referred to there is a blackish limestone, about one foot thick, interstratified with serpentine. Dr. Hunt, while examining these rocks, had a portion of the limestone sliced for examination under the microscope, which revealed a structure resembling that of some coral. The serpentines, which are dark colored, opaque, and contain much disseminated magnetic iron, yield by analysis considerable portions of chrome and traces of nickel. On an island opposite the portage, the rock is blackish-blue hard slate, rarely with what appear to be small grains of whitish feldspar. On the various portages and small lakes passed over from this point to Lake Wakinitche, the only rock seen is chloritic slate. The same remark applies also to the lake itself, from its south-west end, along the south-east side, to within six miles of its outlet. In this last distance, and for a mile beyond the outlet, only conglomerate rocks are seen. These resemble the two varieties already described. On the north-west side of the lake, about the middle, these rocks rise to a height of 150 or 200 feet, forming a bare escarpment, extending for about four miles; and, on the same side, near the outlet, Wakinitche

Mountain, which is entirely composed of them, rises about 350 to 400 feet high, for the most part bare and rocky, and extending along the margin of the lake for nearly three miles. The fragments in the conglomerates in the last localities are chiefly of Laurentian rocks, and the enclosed masses are often many tons in weight. In some parts, without close examination, the conglomerate might be mistaken for Laurentian gneiss. In many parts of this hill considerable exposures of red shale are met with, as well as grey and chocolate-brown sandstones made up of fine grains of reddish feldspar and white quartz. Although lines of deposition were observable in these sandstones, I could trace no regular line of strike or dip."

On the Little Perch River, which flows into Chabestachuan Bay, and three miles from its mouth, Mr. McOuat met with some small exposures of a reddish feldspathic rock, apparently of a brecciated character, with calcareous seams, and showing a considerable amount of a dull green steatitic mineral. This rock occupies, as nearly as possible, the position in which one might expect to meet with Mr. Richardson's group, and may represent some of the conglomerates of that group. Nothing was seen at all like the chloritic slates of Lakes Wakinichi and Chibogomon. The above band is not over one mile wide, coming in between the Laurentian gneiss and the Cambrian limestone.

Little Perch River.

Farther to the eastward, on the Temiscamie River, I failed to find any trace of these rocks, and am of the opinion that the belt does not extend that far to the eastward.

The following is the description of the economic minerals found in these rocks, as given by Mr. Richardson :—

Copper.

"*Copper.*—Copper pyrites has already been mentioned as occurring in the neighborhood of Paint Mountain, on Lake Abatagomaw. At a point a little to the south-west of the mountain, on the lake shore, this ore is met with in specks, together with stains of the green carbonate, but no well-defined bed or vein was observed. The rock a green, slightly calcareous, chloritic slate. These indications of copper are seen for nearly half-a-mile north-easterly along the lake shore, to another point, where a bed or vein, two feet thick, containing copper-pyrites, is seen in chloritic rock for about twenty feet. Its strike is N. 31 E., and S. 31° E., the underlie not being determinable. The portion of the vein exposed would probably yield four or five per cent. of copper throughout, while parts of it might produce ten or twelve per cent. For about three-quarters of a mile farther along the shore, specks of the yellow sulphuret and the green carbonate of copper are met with wherever the rock appears. At the end of this distance, and just under Paint Mountain, the rock is largely charged with fine-grained iron-pyrites and specks of yellow sulphuret, in a yellowish quartzose gangue. Here the iron-pyrites constitutes as much as fifteen or twenty per cent. of the rock, while along the whole of the distance above described, about one and a-quarter miles, it is never absent, though occurring in small quantities. At the last mentioned place is the depression before described. As before stated, it is filled with drift, and no rock is seen in it; but from the quantities of iron and copper-pyrites met with in the rock on both sides of it, it is quite possible that under the drift a valuable deposit of copper ore may exist.

"*Iron.*—About half-a-mile south-west of the first mentioned copper ore, and near the lake shore, there is a deposit of magnetic iron ore in chlorite slate; its breadth is fifty feet, and it is seen on its strike, which is S. 65° W., and N. 65° E., about 200 paces. The ore occurs in crystalline lumps and grains throughout the rock. The whole fifty feet would probably yield an average of from fifteen to twenty per cent. of iron. Iron.

"*Ochre.*—The only place this was observed was in the north-east part of Paint Mountain, where a small deposit was met with about half way up the mountain, which probably derives its name from the presence of this ochre or paint." Ochre.

CAMBRIAN.

The limestones found on Lakes Mistassini and Mistassinis, owing to the absence of any fossil remains, have been referred to this horizon on account of their lithological resemblance to Cambrian rocks of the east side of James Bay.

These rocks form the basin of the two lakes, and extend but little beyond their shore line. The south-west boundary is at the end of Abatigoush Bay, where they succeed the Huronian rocks seen on Lake Wakiniche, the contact of the formations being concealed by drift. Area.

Following the western limit, we next find the limestones in contact with, and lying unconformably on, the Laurentian gneiss, on Ponichuan Bay, at the place where the bay narrows. The boundary then follows along the north-west shore of the lake to the north-east end, and I think continues in the same course to a low range of hills, which lies about ten miles beyond the end of the lake.

Sweeping eastward along the base of these hills, the rocks extend beyond the south-west side of Lake Mistassinis, and are seen to occupy the whole of that shore.

Mr. Bignell describes the limestones as occurring several miles on the Temiscamie River, from its inlet to Lake Mistassinis.

These rocks have a strike parallel, approximately, to the length of the lakes, the dip being to the south, and changing to eastward at the Dip. southern end of the lake, with an angle varying from 4° to 10°. The lower beds resting unconformably on the gneiss, at the western side of Lake Mistassini, are made up of a dark bluish-grey limestone, holding concretionary masses of dark blue chert, with thin bands of black argillaceous shale. Above this are thin beds of light blue fine-grained dolomitic limestone, weathering yellow, interbedded with thin layers of a greyish, coarse, gritty limestone, containing large quantities of sand. Next, a ten-feet bed of massive light blue, pure limestone very compact and hard. This rock is traversed by deep vertical cracks, probably due to the action of frost. Overlying this bed are thinner ones of the same character, intermingled with beds of coarse, grey silicious limestone, full of grit.

The top layer is a limestone conglomerate, made up of limestone pebbles embedded in a sandy matrix.

The thickness of the whole series does not exceed one hundred feet.

Although closely examined, none of the above beds gave any evidence of fossil remains, the supposed fossils found by Mr. Richardson having, on closer examination, proved to be only mineral concretions.

Superficial Deposits.

Owing to the absence of any considerable elevations near the sea coast, and to the shallow valleys cut by the rivers, but little information was obtained relating to the drift deposits.

Where good rock exposures occurred, they were generally formed by having the usual covering of vegetable matter burnt away, and the heat occasioned by this, along with subsequent rains, has been sufficient to obliterate any traces of glacial striation. Thus the direction of the drift can only be arrived at by a study of the travelled boulders. In the vicinity of Lake Mistassini, no rounded boulders of limestone were met with in directions to the east and north-west of the lake, and the probability is that the drift there was from north-east to south-west. On the Peribonka River, boulders of green chloritic and epidotic rocks were seen. These are supposed not to have come from the rocks of Lake Wakiniche, but from a similar patch of Huronian rocks, which, I am told, occurs near the head-waters of the Outard and Maniquagan Rivers, to the north-east of the place where the boulders were seen.

No exposures of boulder-clay were seen, although the surface of the whole country is thickly covered with rounded, travelled boulders, both great and small, showing the action of ice.

As before mentioned, on the Betsiamites River, at intervals along its shores, as far as the first fall, beds of blue clay were seen overlaid by sand. In places the exposures of these showed a thickness of thirty feet of clay, and the beds were greatly crumpled and folded.

The surrounding country here is too low to afford good illustrations of terraces and none were seen. Beyond the first fall, and as far as Lake Mistassini, the banks of the rivers and lakes passed are low, and no good cuttings in the drift were seen.

Three miles to the north of the Hudson Bay post on Lake Mistassini, is a sand-bank forty feet high, without signs of stratification, and containing quantities of coarse gravel. Similar exposures were also seen near the Big Narrows.

On the Rupert River, nothing but sand was seen until the Oatmeal Fall was passed. Below this, the river banks are cut out of a blue clay, showing stratification and overlaid by sand. These clays often show in exposures a thickness of thirty feet, and are very free from boulders.

APPENDIX I.

LIST OF BIRDS COLLECTED AT LAKE MISTASSINI, BY JAS. M. MACOUN, 1885.

Hylocichla mustelina, Baird. Robin. Common. Breeds. May 8th.

Hylocichla Unalashkae, var. *Pallasi*, Ridgw. Hermit Thrush. Not rare. Breeds. May 23rd.

Regulus calendula, Licht. Ruby-crowned Kinglet. Common. Breeds. May 11th.

Parus atricapillus, L. Chickadee. During winter.

Anorthura (Troglodytes) hyemalis, Coues. Winter Wren. During winter.

Helminthophaga peregrina, Baird. Tennessee Warbler. Not rare. Breeds. June 13th

Dendroeca aestiva, Baird. Yellow-bird. Common. Breeds. May 30th.

Dendroeca maculosa, Baird. Magnolia Warbler. Not rare. Breeds. May 25th.

Dendroeca striata, Baird. Black-Poll Warbler. Not rare. Breeds. June 15th.

Siurus naevius, Coues. Water Thrush. Breeds here. Common. May 19th.

Wilsonia pusilla Bp., Green. Black-capped Yellow Warbler. Not rare. Breeds. May 30th.

Tachycineta bicolor, Caban. White-bellied Swallow. Common. Breeds. May 10th.

Ampelis cedorum, Baird. Cedar Bird. Rare. Breeds.

Pinicola enucleator, Vieill. Pine Grosbeak. During winter.

Loxia leucoptera, Gm. White-winged Cross-bill. During winter.

Ægiothus linaria, Caban. Common Red-poll. During winter.

Plectrophanes nivalis, Meyer. Snow Bunting. Leave about May 10th.

Melospiza fasciata, Scott. Song Sparrow. Common. Breeds. May 23rd.

Junco hyemalis, Scl. Black Snow-bird. All year, and breeds.

Spizella montana, Ridgw. Tree Sparrow. Common. Breeds. May 15th.

Zonotrichia albicollis, Bon. White-throated Sparrow. Common. Breeds. May 20th.

Zonotrichia leucophrys, Swains, W. Common. Breeds. May 20th.

Molothrus ater, Gray. Cow-bird. Common. Breeds. May 14th.

Scolecophagus ferrugineus, Sw. Rusty Grackle. Breeds. Common. May 14th.

Corvus corax, var. *carnivorus*, Bartr. Raven. One specimen. May 30th.

Perisoreus Canadensis, Bon. Whiskey Jack. All year. Breeds.

Empidonax flaviventris, Baird. Yellow-bellied Fly-catcher. Common. Breeds. June 2nd.

Chordeiles popetue Baird. Night Hawk. Not rare. Breeds. May 29th.

Ceryle alcyon, Boie. King-fisher. Common. Breeds. May 14th.

Picus pubescens, Linn. Downy Wood-pecker. During winter.

Colaptes auratus, Sw. Golden-winged Woodpecker. Not common. Breeds. June 10th.

Surnia funerea, Rich & Sw. Day-owl. Rare. During winter.

Pandion haliaetus, var. *Carolinensis*, Gmelin. Fish-hawk. Not common. July 10th.

Canace Canadensis, Bon. Spruce Partridge. Common all year.

Bonasa umbellus, Steph. Partridge. Common all year.

Lagopus albus, Aud. Willow Ptarmigan. Appear about Oct. 25th. Depart about May 1st.

Œgialitis semipalmatus, Caban. Semi-palmated Ring-necked Plover. One specimen. May 29th.

Totanus melanoleucus, Vieill. Greater Yellow-legs. A single pair. May 7th.

Totanus flavipes, Vieill. Yellow-legs. A single pair. August 10th.

Rhyacophilus solitarius, Cass. Solitary Sand-piper. Common. Breeds. May 23rd.

Nyctiardea grisea, var. *nævia*, Allen. Night Heron. A single specimen. Aug. 6th.

Bernicla Canadensis, Boie. Canada Goose. Passed May 2nd.

Anas obscura, Gmel. Dusky Duck. Passed May 20th.

Clangula (Glaucium) Americana, Bonap. Golden-eye. Passed. May 3rd.

Somateria spectabilis, Boie. King-Eider Duck. One specimen, Not known before.

Œdemia Americana, Sw. & Rich. Sea-coot. Passed. May 15th.

Œdemia perspicillata, Flem. Surf Duck. Passed. May 28th.

Mergus merganser, var. *Americanus*, Cassin. Sheldrake. Not rare. Breeds. June 1st.

Mergus serrator, Linn. Red-breasted Sheldrake. Not rare. Breeds. May 11th.

Larus Delawarensis, Ord. Ring-billed Gull. Common. Breeds. May 11th

Sterna Forsteri, Nutt. Forster's Tern. Common. Breeds. June 1st.

Colymbus torquatus, Brünn. Great Northern Diver. Common. Breeds. May 14th.

Colymbus arcticus, Linn. Black-throated Diver. Not common. Breeds. June 3rd.

NOTE.—In the above list, the date following each species refers to the day upon which it was first shot, unless otherwise specified.

APPENDIX II.

List of plants collected at Lake Mistassini, Rupert River and Rupert House, by Jas. M. Macoun, 1885.

The first column in the following list contains those species found at Lake Mistassini, the second, the species growing along the Rupert River and not noted at Mistassini, and the third, the species growing at Rupert House and not seen either at Mistassini or along the Rupert.

Nos.		Mistassini.	Rupert River.	Rupert House.
	RANUNCULACEÆ.			
1	Anemone parviflora, Michx	*		
2	" dichotoma, Linn		*	
3	Thalictrum dioicum, L.	*		
4	Ranunculus abortivus, L			*
5	" Cymbalaria, Pursh			*
6	" Pennsylvanicus, L	*		
7	" recurvatus, Poir	*		
8	Caltha palustris, L			*
9	Coptis trifolia, Salisb	*		
10	Actæa spicata L. var. rubra, Ait	*		
	NYMPHÆACEÆ.			
11	Nuphar advena, Ait	*		
	SARRACENIACEÆ.			
12	Sarracenia purpurea, L	*		
	FUMARIACEÆ.			
13	Corydalis glauca, Pursh		*	
	CRUCIFERÆ.			
14	Nasturtium palustre, D. C	*		
15	Cardamine hirsuta, L	*		
16	" pratensis, L	*		
17	Capsella Bursa-pastoris, Moench	*		
18	Thlaspi arvense, L			*
	VIOLACEÆ.			
19	Viola cucullata, Ait	*		
20	Viola canina L. var. sylvestris, Reg	*		

No.		Mistassini.	Rupert River.	Rupert House.
	CARYOPHYLLACEÆ.			
21	Silene noctiflora, L			*
22	" Armeria, L			*
23	Arenaria Michauxii, Hook	*		
24	Stellaria media, Smith			*
25	" borealis Bigel. var. alpestris, Gray	*		
26	" humifusa, Rottb	*		
27	" longipes, Goldie			*
28	Cerastium arvense, L		*	
	GERANIACEÆ.			
29	Geranium Carolinianum, L		*	
	RHAMNACEÆ.			
30	Rhamnus alnifolius, L'Her	*		
	LEGUMINOSÆ.			
31	Vicia Cracca, L			*
32	" Americana, Muhl			*
	ROSACEÆ.			
33	Prunus Pennsylvanica, L	*		
34	Spiræa salicifolia, L	*		
35	Geum macrophyllum, Willd	*		
36	" rivale, L	*		
37	" strictum, Ait		*	
38	Fragaria Virginiana, Ehrh	*		
39	Potentilla Norvegica, L	*		
40	" arguta, Pursh	*		
41	" Anserina, L	*		
42	" fruticosa, L	*		
43	" tridentata, Ait	*		
44	" palustris, Scop	*		
45	" Pennsylvanica, L			*
46	Rubus Chamæmorus, L	*		
47	" triflorus, Rich	*		
48	" arcticus, L	*		
49	" " var. grandiflorus, Ledeb	*		
50	" strigosus, Michx	*		
51	Rosa Sayii, Wat	*		
52	Pyrus Americana, D C			
53	Amelanchier Canadensis, T. & G., var. oblongifolia, T. & G.	*		
54	" " var. oligocarpa, T. & G.	*		
	SAXIFRAGACEÆ.			
55	Mitella nuda, L	*		
56	Parnassia palustris, L			*
57	Ribes lacustre, Poir	*		
58	" prostratum, L'Her	*		
59	" rubrum, L	*		
60	" oxycanthoides, L	*		

No.		Mistassini	Rupert River.	Rupert House.
	DROSERACEÆ.			
61	Drosera rotundifolia, L.	*		
62	" intermedia Drev. & Hayne, var. Americana, DC.	*		
	HALORAGEÆ.			
63	Hippuris vulgaris, L.	*		
	ONAGRACEÆ.			
64	Circæa alpina, L			*
65	Epilobium angustifolium, L.	*		
66	" palustre L. var. lineare, Gr.	*		
67	" tetragonum, L.	*		
	UMBELLIFERÆ.			
68	Sanicula Marilandica, L.	*		
69	Heracleum lanatum, Michx	*		
70	Archangelica atropurpurea, Hoffm			*
71	Cicuta maculata, L.		*	
	ARALIACEÆ.			
72	Aralia hispida, Michx	*		
73	Aralia nudicaulis, L.	*		
	CORNACEÆ.			
74	Cornus Canadensis, L.	*		
75	" sericea, L.		*	
76	" stolonifera, Michx	*		
	CAPRIFOLIACEÆ.			
77	Linnæa borealis, Gronov	*		
78	Lonicera involucrata, Banks	*		
79	" cærulea, L	*		
80	Diervilla trifida, Moench	*		
81	Sambucus pubens, Michx	*		
82	Viburnum pauciflorum, Pylaie	*		
	RUBIACEÆ.			
83	Galium triflorum, Michx	*		
84	" trifidum, L.	*		
85	" asprellum, Michx		*	
	VALERIANACEÆ.			
86	Valeriana sylvatica, Rich	*		
87				
88	**COMPOSITÆ.**			
89				
90	Eupatorium purpureum, L.		*	
91	Solidago lanceolata, L.		*	
92	" Canadensis, L.	*		
93	" bicolor, L. var. concolor, T. & G.		*	

No.		Mistassini.	Rupert River.	Rupert House.
94	Solidago uliginosa, Nutt	*		
95	" macrophylla, Pursh	*		
96	Aster Lindleyanus, T. & G.	*		
97	" puniceus, L		*	
98	" salicifolius, Ait			*
99	" umbellatus, Mill, var. villosus		*	
100	" nemoralis, Ait		*	
101	Erigeron hyssopifolius, Michx	*		
102	" Canadensis, L		*	
103	" Philadelphicus, L		*	
104	Antennaria plantaginifolia, Hook	*		
105	Anaphalis margaritacea, Benth. & Hook	*		
106	Bidens frondosa, L			*
107	" cernua, L			*
108	Achillæa millefolium, L	*		
109	Petasites palmata, Gray	*		
110	" sagittata, Gray			*
111	Senecio aureus, L	*		
112	" " var. obovatus, T. & G	*		
113	" vulgaris, L			*
114	Cnicus muticus, Pursh	*		
115	Hieracium umbellatum, Linn		*	
116	" scabrum, Michx		*	
117	Taraxacum officinale, Web. var. lividum, Koch	*		
118	Lactuca leucophæa, Gray	*		
119	Prenanthes alba, Linn	*		
120	" racemosa, Hook			*
	LOBELIACEÆ.			
121	Lobelia Dortmanna, Linn		*	
122	" Kalmii, L	*		
	CAMPANULACEÆ.			
123	Campanula rotundifolia, L	*		
	VACCINIACEÆ.			
124	Vaccinium Canadense, Kalm	*		
125	" uliginosum, L	*		
126	" Pennsylvanicum, L	*		
127	Oxycoccus vulgaris, Pursh	*		
128	" macrocarpus, Pursh	*		
129	Chiogenes hispidula, T. & G	*		
	ERICACEÆ.			
130	Arctostaphylos Uva-ursi, Spreng	*		
131	Epigæa repens, L	*		
132	Cassandra calyculata, Don	*		
133	Andromeda polifolia, L	*		
134	Kalmia glauca, Ait	*		
135	" angustifolia, L	*		
136	Ledum latifolium, Ait	*		
137	Pyrola secunda, L	*		
138	" rotundifolia, L. var. uliginosa, Gray	*		
139	Moneses uniflora, Gray	*		

No.		Mistassini.	Rupert River.	Rupert House.
	Primulaceæ.			
140	Primula Mistassinica, Michx	*		
141	Trientalis Americana, Pursh	*		
142	Lysimachia stricta, Ait		*	
	Lentibulaceæ.			
143	Utricularia vulgaris, L	*		
144	" intermedia, Hayne..........	*		
145	Pinguicula vulgaris, L..			
	Apocynaceæ.			
146	Apocynum androsæmifolium, L.................. .		*	
	Gentianaceæ.			
147	Gentiana serrata, Gunner................			*
148	" linearis, Froel............		*	
149	Menyanthes trifoliata, L............			
	Borraginaceæ.			
150	Myosotis verna, Nutt..............................		*	
	Scrophulariaceæ.			
151	Mimulus ringens, L....		*	
152	Veronica Americana, Schw	*		
153	Castilleia pallida, Kunth..........................			*
154	Euphrasia officinalis, L.....			*
155	Rhinanthus Crista-galli, L...........	*		
156	Pedicularis palustris, L. var..........................			*
157	Melampyrum Americanum, Michx...........	*		
	Labiatæ.			
158	Mentha Canadensis, L	*		
159	Lycopus sinuatus, Gray		*	
160	Dracocephalum parviflorum, Nutt....................		*	
161	Brunella vulgaris, L..................................	*		
162	Scutellaria galericulata, L	*		
163	" lateriflora, L.........................			*
164	Galeopsis Tetrahit, L............			*
165	Stachys palustris, L..................................			*
166	Lamium amplexicaule, L..............................			*
	Plantaginaceæ.			
167	Plantago major, L.................		*	
	Chenopodiaceæ.			
168	Chenopodium album, L..	*		

No.		Mistassini.	Rupert River.	Rupert House.
	POLYGONACEÆ.			
169	Polygonum aviculare, L.	*		
170	" amphibium, L	*		
171	" cilinode, Michx	*		
172	" viviparum		*	
173	" lapathifolium, Ait. var. incanum, Hook		*	
174	Rumex verticillatus, L			*
	SANTALACEÆ.			
175	Comandra livida, Rich	*		
	URTICACEÆ.			
176	Urtica gracilis, Ait		*	
	MYRICACEÆ.			
177	Myrica Gale, L	*		
	BETULACEÆ.			
178	Betula pumila, L	*		
179	" papyracea, Ait	*		
180	" lutea, Michx, f.	*		
181	Alnus viridis, D. C	*		
182	" incana, Willd	*		
	SALICACEÆ.			
183	Salix candida, Willd	*		
184	" desertorum, Rich	*		
185	" myrtilloides, L	*		
186	" glauca, L	*		
187	" discolor, Muhl	*		
188	Populus tremuloides, Michx	*		
189	" balsamifera, L	*		
190	Pinus Banksiana, Lamb	*		
	CONIFERÆ.			
191	Abies balsamea, Marsh	*		
192	Picea alba, Link	*		
193	" nigra, Link	*		
194	Larix Americana, Michx	*		
195	Thuja occidentalis, L	*		
196	Taxus baccata, L. var. Canadensis, Gr	*		
197	Juniperus communis, L	*		
	ORCHIDACEÆ.			
198	Habenaria dilatata, Gray	*		
199	" hyperborea, Lindl	*		
200	" obtusata, Rich	*		
201	" rotundifolia, Rich	*		
202	Goodyera repens, R. Br	*		
203	Spiranthes Romanzoviana, Cham	*		

No.		Mistassini.	Rupert River.	Rupert House.
204	Listera cordata, R. Br	*		
205	" convallarioides, Hook	*		
206	Calypso borealis, Salisb	*		
207	Corallorhiza innata, R. Br	*		
208	Cypripedium pubescens, Willd	*		
209	" acaule, Ait		*	
	Iridaceæ.			
210	Iris versicolor, L	*		
	Liliaceæ.			
211	Tofieldia glutinosa, Willd	*		
212	" palustris, Huds	*		
213	Streptopus roseus, Michx	*		
214	" amplexifolius, D C.	*		
215	Clintonia borealis, Raf	*		
216	Maianthemum bifolium, D C.	*		
	Juncaceæ.			
217	Luzula spadicea, D. C.	*		
218	Juncus alpinus, Vill. var. insignis, Fries	*		
219	" Canadensis, var. coarctatus, Gr.	*		
220	" filiformis, L.	*		
221	" tenuis, Willd	*		
	Araceæ.			
222	Calla palustris, L.		*	
	Typhaceæ.			
223	Sparganium simplex, Hudson, var. fluitans, Gr.	*		
	Naiadaceæ.			
224	Naias flexilis, Rostk	*		
225	Zannichellia palustris, L	*		
226	Potamogeton gramineus, L. var. graminifolius	*		
227	" " var. heterophyllus, Schreb.	*		
228	" pectinatus, L.	*		
229	" perfoliatus, L	*		
230	" pusillus, L.	*		
231	" rufescens, Schrad	*		
	Alismaceæ.			
232	Triglochin maritimum, L.	*		
	Cyperaceæ.			
233	Scirpus validus, Vahl	*		
234	" microcarpus, Presl			*
235	Eriophorum alpinum, L			
236	" vaginatum, L			

No.		Mistassini.	Rupert River.	Rupert House.
237	Carex angustata, Boott			
238	" arctata, Boott			
239	" atrata, L	*		
240	" aurea, Nutt	*		
241	" Buxbaumii, Wahl	*		
242	" canescens, L	*		
243	" " var. alpicola	*		
244	" capillaris, L	*		
245	" chordorhiza, Ehrh	*		
246	" concinna, R. Br	*		
247	" echinata, Murr	*		
248	" flava, L	*		
249	" flexilis, Rudge	*		
250	" lenticularis, Michx	*		
251	" maritima, Vahl			*
252	" miliaris, Michx	*		
253	" Magellanica, Lam	*		
254	" monile, Tuck	*		
255	" Œderi, Ehrh		*	
256	" oligosperma, Michx	*		
257	" polytrichoides, Muhl	*		
258	" scoparia, Schk	*		
259	" teretiuscula, Good		*	
260	" utriculata, Schk	*		
261	" vaginata, Tausch			
	GRAMINEÆ.			
262	Beckmannia eruceæformis, Host			*
263	Panicum dichotomum, L		*	
264	Alopecurus geniculatus var. aristulatus, Monro, L		*	
265	Hierochloa borealis, R. & S	*		
266	Stipa Richardsonii, Link		*	
267	Oryzopsis asperifolia, Michx	*		
268	Phleum pratense, L	*		
269	Agrostis scabra, Willd	*		
270	Deyeuxia Canadensis, Beaur	*		
271	" neglecta, Kth	*		
272	Deschampsia atropurpurea, Wahl	*		
273	" cæspitosa, Beaur	*		
274	" flexuosa, L	*		
275	Poa pratensis, L	*		
276	Glyceria Canadensis, Trin		*	
277	" nervata, Trin	*		
278	Bromus ciliatus, L			
279	Agropyrum tenerum, Vasey	*		
280	Hordeum jubatum, L			*
	EQUISETACEÆ.			
281	Equisetum arvense, L	*		
282	" palustre, L	*		
283	" scirpoides, Michx	*		
	FILICES.			
284	Polypodium vulgare, L	*		
285	Pellæa gracilis, Hook			

No.		Mistassini.	Rupert River.	Rupert House.
286	Pteris aquilina, L			
287	Asplenium viride, Hudson	*		
288	" Filix-foemina, Bernh	*		
289	Phegopteris Dryopteris, Fée	*		
290	" calcarea, R. Br	*		
291	Aspidium spinulosum var. dilatatum, Gr	*		
292	Onoclea sensibilis, L		*	
293	Cystopteris fragilis, Bernh			
294	" montana, Bernh	*		
295	Woodsia Ilvensis, R. Br	*		
296	" glabella, R. Br	*		
297	Osmunda regalis, L	*		
298	" Claytoniana, L	*		
299	Botrychium Lunaria, Swz	*		
300	" Virginicum, Swz	*		
301	" ternatum, Swz. var lunarioides, Milde		*	

LYCOPODIACEÆ.

No.		Mistassini.	Rupert River.	Rupert House.
302	Lycopodium annotinum, L	*		
303	" dendroideum, Michx	*		
304	" clavatum, L	*		
305	" complanatum, L	*		
306	" " var. sabinæfolium, Sp	*		

APPENDIX III.

METEOROLOGICAL OBSERVATIONS TAKEN ON THE ROUTE FROM BETSIAMITES TO LAKE MISTASSINI, AND AT THE HUDSON BAY POST, MISTASSINI, AUGUST 8TH, 1884 TO AUGUST, 21ST, 1885.

The readings are those of a mercurial barometer until December 17th, after that date a small aneroid was used.

The temperature is stated in degrees Farenheit.

The force of the wind is estimated according to Beaufort's scale. The proportion of sky covered by clouds is estimated on a scale of 0 to 10, 0 being a cloudless sky, 10 an overcast sky. The character of the clouds is denoted by the usual letters or combinations of letters referring to Howard's classification.

LOCALITY.	Date.	Thermometer.			Barometer.			Maximum.	Minimum.	Wind. Direction.			Wind. Force.			Weather.			Remarks.
	Aug.	7	2	9	7	2	9			7	2	9	7	2	9	7	2	9	
Betsiamites	1				29.43					S.W.						4 C.3.			
"	2																		
"	3																		
"	4																		
"	5																		
"	6																		
"	7																		
"	8	60		52	30.08		30.15			N.W.		0			0	Haze.		Clear.	
13 miles up Betsiamites River	9	51		62	30.28		30.21			0		0			0	0		0	
25 " " "	10	67		61	30.14		29.95			W.		0	1		0	5 K.S.		0	
30 " " "	11	49		67	29.98		29.90			W.		0	1		0	0		0	
1st Fall, Betsiamites River	12	61		63	30.18		30.05			0		0	0		0	0		0	
9 miles above 1st Fall	13	49		59	30.10		29.90			0		0	0		0	Fog.		0	
15 " "	14	61		62	29.90		29.59			0		0	0		0	0		S.S.	
18 " "	15	60		50	29.68		29.64			W.		0	1		0	2 K.S.		0	
20 " "	16	55		65	29.72		29.50			W.		0	1		0	0		0	
20 " "	17	68		68	29.54		29.38			0		W.	0		3	0		0	
20 " "	18	62		54	29.50		28.61			W.		0	3		0	5 S.		0	
20 " "	19	70			28.40		28.70			W.			3			10 S.		N.	
35 " "	20			64	28.83		28.69			W.		0	2		0	0		0	
30 " "	21	77			28.65		28.50			S.W.		0	1		0	5 K.S.		10 S.	
30 " "	22			57	28.57		28.60					W.			1	10 S.		3 K.S.	

55 miles above 1st Fall	Aug. 23	55		52	28.63		28.43					N.W.				10 S.		10 S.	
70 " "	24	47			28.40		28.60			E.		E.	1		1	N.		N.	
70 " "	25	44		48	28.82		28.87			W.		0	1		0	0		10 S.	
Lake Pipmuakin	26	44		51	28.61		28.50			W.		W.	5		5	N.		5 K.S.	
" "	27	41			28.70		28.68			W.		0	3		0	5 K.S.		0	
70 miles above 1st Fall	28				28.60		28.62			W.		0			0	N.		Fog.	
70 " "	29				28.57		28.49			W.		W.				6 S.		0	
70 " "	30						28.36			E.		0	1		0	N.		5 K.S.	
70 " "	31									E.		E.				N.		N.	
	Sept.																		
70 " "	1															10 S.			
70 " "	2															N.			
70 " "	3															N.	N.	N.	
70 " "	4															0	0	0	
70 " "	5															0	0	0	
39 " "	6															10 S.	10 S.	N.	
39 " "	7															0		0	
60 " "	8															0	0	0	
70 " "	9																		
70 " "	10									E.						0		0	
Lake Pipmuakin	11									E.		W.			4	N.		0	
" "	12								40	N.W.		N.W.	4		4	0		0	
" "	13								37	N.W.		N.W.	4		4	0		0	
" "	14								34	N.W.		N.W.	4		4				
" "	15			37			28.56		27	W.		W.	3		1	0		0	
" "	16	39		49	28.58		28.00		34	E.		E.	1		3	N.	N.	N.	
" "	17	50			28.15		28.19		34	W.		W.	2		1	6 K.S.		5 K.S.	
" "	18	35		31	28.70		28.92		33	N.W.		0	2		0	2 K.S.		0	
" "	19	33		31	29.04		28.88		29	0		0	0		0	Fog.		0	
Pipmuakin River	20	40		42	28.66		28.69		25	E.		W.	1		1	N.	N.	N.	
" "	21	42		46	28.86		28.56		39	0		E.	0		1	Haze.		10 S.	
" "	22	43		29	28.44		28.51		42	N.W.		0	3		0			0	
Manouan Portage	23	25		24	28.66		28.73		22			0			0			0	
" "	24	37			28.62		28.17		21	0		E.	0		1	10 S.	10 S.	N.	
Manouan River	25			38	28.49		28.70			W.		W.	4		3	10 S.		0	
" "	26	34		39	28.98		28.78		31	W.		0	3		0	5 K.S.		10 S.	
" "	27	42			28.51		28.16		29			S.				7 S.		N.	
" "	28				28.37		28.25			W.		0	1		0	5 K.S.		10 S.	
" "	29				27.85		28.14			S.W.		S.W.	1		4	N.		N.	
" "	30	43		42	28.53		28.42			W.		E.	4		1	N.		N.	
	Oct.																		
Lake Manouan Portage	1	37		34	28.41		28.58		35	W.		W.	1		3	10 S.		10 S.	Rained in showers all day.
" "	2	30		25	28.82		28.82		27			N.			3	10 S.		0	Aurora (3) last night.
" "	3	20		32	28.75		28.36		14	0		E.			2	Haze.		N.	
Lake Manouan	4	34		38	28.00		28.02		31	W.		W.	2		1	N.		9 S.	About 1 in. snow during night.
" "	5	35		34	28.35		28.40		31	W.		N.	2		1			0	
" "	6	34		37	28.35		28.20		28	N.E.		0	3		0	2 C.			Rn. from 9 to 2, snow till 6.30, (3 inches.)
" "	7	34			28.25		28.25		29	N.		0	1		0	10 S.		0	

LOCALITY.	Date	Thermometer.			Barometer.			Maximum.	Minimum.	Wind. Direction.			Wind. Force.			Weather.			Remarks.
	Oct.	7	2	9	7	2	9			7	2	9	7	2	9	7	2	9	
Lake Manouan	8	...	...	...	28.10	...	27.96		...	0	...	0	0	.	1	10 S.	N.	N.	Snow, 1 inch.
" "	9	...	...	31	28.25	...	28.15		...	N.W.	N.W.	N.W.	3	3	3	0	0	0	
" "	10	34		34	28.28	.	28.22	...	20	N.W.	N.W.	N.W.	3	3	3	5 K.S.	10 S.	10 S.	
" "	11	...	...	47	27.92	...	27.84	...	...	S.W.	S.W.	S.W.	2-4	2-4	2-4	10 S.	N.	N.	Rained during day
" "	12	...	...	...	...	...	...	..	32	...	...	...				10 S.	...	...	
" "	13	35	...	33	28.21	...	28.31	..	32	W.	W.	W.	3	3	3	10 S.	10 S.	10 S.	
Peribonka portage	14	34		28	28.57	...	28.50	..	21	...	...	...						..	
Peribonka River	15	24	...	25	28.37	..	28.59	...	23	W.	W.	W.	1	1	1	0	0	0	Aurora (2) last night
" "	16	27		..	28.32	...	27.96		..	S.W.	S.W.	S.W.	3	3	3	N.	N.	N.	Snow and rain showers
" "	17	31	...	27	27.98	...	28.03	...	28	W.	W.	W.	1	1	1	7 S.	..	5 S.	Snow and rain during night
" "	18	24		23	28.13	...	28.38	...	24	W.	W.	0	1	1	0	10 S.	10 S.	Haze.	Snow flurries during the day
" "	19	25			28.57	...	28.29	...	18	W.	W.	S.W.	1	1	1	N.	N.	N.	Snow with rain following
Peribonka branch	20	28		..	28.01	...	28.60	...	24	W.	W.	W.	3	4	2	N.	N.	0	Rain in the morning
" "	21	19	..	..	28.88	...	28.18	..	19	W.	W.	N.W.	1	1	3	0	0	10 S.	
" "	22	33	...	31	27.90	...	27.98	...	25	W.	W.	W.	1	1	1	N.	N.	10 S.	Rain and snow
Winter Camp on Branch	23	25	.	21	28.12	...	28.27	...	24	W.	W.	0	1	1	0	N.	N.	10 S.	Snow flurries during the day
" " "	24	10	22	18	28.12	28.36	28.42	23	12	0	E.	N.	0	1	3	9 S.	N.	N.	Snow. Lake partly frozen over
" " "	25	22	28	21	28.37	28.38	28.40	30	17	0	0	0	0	0	0	N.	N.	N.	First ptarmigans seen
" " "	26	02	21	21	28.81	28.83	28.58	20	01	W.	0	0	1	0	0	0	9 S.	N.	Snow during night
" " "	27	24	20	32	28.35	28.22	28.13	32	18	S.W.	W.	W.	3	4	1	N.	N.	10 S.	6 inches of snow
" " "	28	31	33	12	28.02	28.07	28.46	36	32	0	W.	0	0	1	0	N.	N.	0	Rain and snow
" " "	29	03	18	12	28.72	28.74	28.74	29	03	0	E.	E.	0	2	2	0	N.	5 K.S.	Aurora (1) last night
" " "	30	04	19	10	28.74	28.65	28.60		05	0	0	0	0	0	0	0	N.	N.	2 inches of snow
" " "	31	18	26	25	28.56	28.49	28.45	...	16	...	...					N.	10 S.	10 S.	1 inch of snow during night
	Nov.																		
1st Lake on Branch	1	24	29	29	28.32	28.21	28.15	30	23	E.	S.E.	S.E.	1	1	1	10 S.	N.	N.	½ inch of snow
" "	2	19	28	25	28.21	28.28	28.45	30	18	0	0	0	0	0	0	5 K.S.	6 S.	10 S.	1 inch of snow during night
" "	3	17	22	14	28.60	28.63	28.65	28	16	W.	W.	0	1	1	0	N.	N.	8 K.S.	Light snow flurries
" "	4	01	20	07	28.80	28.42	28.78	21	08	W.	0	0	1	0	0	Haze.	7 K.S.	Haze.	
" "	5	13	14	11	28.08	28.08	27.82	16	02	N.E.	N.E.	N.E.	1	3	2	N.	N.	N.	4 inches of snow during day
" "	6	08	17	09	27.69	27.60	28.12	16	08	N.E.	N.W.	N.	3	3	1	10 S.	5 K.S.	0	2 inches of snow during night
" "	7	01	11	07	28.10	27.92	27.94	11	00	0	N.E.	0	0	3	0	10 S.	N.	N.	Snowing lightly all day
" "	8	13	17	05	28.21	28.36	28.47	17	13	0	0	0	0	0	0	0	0	0	
" "	9	25	13	13	28.51	28.50	28.40	14	25	0	0	0	0	0	0	0	10 S.	10 S.	
" "	10	19	27	29	28.45	28.30	28.30	30	13	0	0	0	0	0	0	10 S.	10 S.	10 S.	
" "	11	33	34	25	28.13	28.04	28.08	35	29	W.	S.W.	W.	1	3	1	N.	9 S.	N.	Rain and snow all day
" "	12	13	16	02	28.33	28.38	28.35	18	13	0	0	0	0	0	0	10 S.	2 C.	0	
" "	13	13	25	21	27.99	27.99	28.00	20	04	S.E.	E.	N.E.	1	2	3	N.	N.	N.	1 inch of snow during day

1st Lake on Branch	14	19	24	24	28.04	.....	27.77	25	18	W.	W.	W.	2	5	5	10 S.	N.	N.	2 in snow. Strong W. gales
„ „	15	10	14	16	28.27	28.36	28.31	17	10	N.	N.W.	0	3	2	0	10 S.	5 K.S.	10 S.	
„ „	16	16	25	19	28.15	28.14	28.19	28	06	0	W.	0	6	1	0	5 K.S.	10 S.	10 S.	
„ „	17	10	07	05	28.15	28.15	28.36	11	06	E.	E.	0	1	1	0	N.	N.	10 S.	2 inches of snow.
„ „	18	04	10	07	28.50	28.50	28.59	11	05	0	N.W.	W.	0	3	2	Haze.	10 S.	10 S.	
„ „	19	02	10	13	28.66	28.66	28.65	13	02	0	W.	0	0	2	0	Haze.	5 K.S.	0	
„ „	20	27	08	12	28.58	28.52	28.38	13	27	0	W.	0	0	1	0	0	0	N.	
„ „	21	14	21	08	28.15	28.15	28.35	23	12	0	W.	N.W.	0	2	3	N.	Haze.	10 S.	3 inches of snow during night.
„ „	22	04	10	00	28.62	28.70	28.78	10	03	N.W.	N.W.	0	5	5	0	5 K.S.	7 S.	10 S.	
„ „	23	00	10	18	28.58	28.30	27.93	19	09	0	0	S.E.	0	0	3	10 S.	10 S.	N.	Snow and hail, 1 inch.
„ „	24	32	05	05	27.43	27.55	27.77	34	24	E.	N.W.	N.W.	3	4	3	N.	N.	0	Rain and sleet all night.
„ „	25	19	01	09	27.91	27.90	27.69	13	21	0	N.W.	0	0	1	0	0	Haze.	N.	
„ „	26	05	12	11	27.70	27.70	27.78	13	05	0	N.W.	0	0	2	0	5 K.S.	10 S.	N.	1 inch of snow during night.
3rd Lake on Branch	27	14	...	04	27.86	......	27.98	....	14	0	W.	W.	0	2	2	0	3 S. 2 St.	0	
„ „	28	01	....	10	27.08	......	27.90	....	14	0	0	0	0	0	0	10 S.	10 S.	0	
„ „	29	01	09	06	27.80	27.73	27.80	....	24	0	0	W.	0	0	3	9 S.	10 S.	10 S.	
5th Lake on Branch	30	12	00	00	28.08	28.03	28.04	....	13	0	W.	W.	0	3	3	2 S.	10 K.S.	N.	
	Dec.																		
„ „	1	06	....	11	28.10	.....	28.02	....	01	W.	S.W.	0	3	3	0	N.	N.	10 S.	Snowing lightly all day.
„ „	2	14	22	24	28.04	27.95	27.76	24	09	0	S.W.	S.W.	0	5	5	Fog.	10 S.	10 S.	Mild and overcast, gale S. W.
„ „	3	26	31	29	27.65	27.60	27.84	....	24	S.W.	S.W.	S.W.	3	3	1	10 S.	N.	N.	Light snow night and day. ¼ in.
„ „	4	26	....	05	27.70	.....	28.03	....	26	S.W.	W.	W.	3	4	1	N.	10 S.	9 S.	Light snow and rain.
Cross Lake	5	19	01	11	28.18	28.21	28.32	....	19	0	0	0	0	0	0	0	0	0	
„	6	03	11	15	28.26	28.23	28.20	....	15	N.E.	E.	0	1	2	0	N.	10 S.	10 S.	Light snow betw'n 7 and 8 a.m.
„	7	21	21	23	27.00	27.46	27.38	....	13	N.E.	E.	E.	5	5	2	N.	N.	N.	5 inches snow with gale from E.
„	8	17	20	16	27.56	27.63	27.71	....	15	0	W.	0	0	1	0	10 S.	10 S.	10 S.	
Height of Land	9	09	....	01	27.80	27.93	......	....	09	W.	W.	W.	1	3	1	10 S.	10 S.	....	Light flurries of snow.
Lake Tamiscamie	10	06	....	25	27.99	......	28.48	....	....	0	W.	0	0	1	0	0	0	C	Aurora (3) to-night.
Crooked Lake	11	25	....	07	28.43	......	28.42	....	28	0	E.	0	0	2	0	5 K.S.	Haze.	0	Aurora (1).
Tamiscamie River	12	03	....	04	28.60	......	28.86	....	08	N.W.	W.	0	2	3	0	10 S.	5 S.	0	
Lake Mistassini	13	28	....	04	28.88	......	28.76	....	31	0	0	0	0	0	0	0	0	10 S.	
„ „	14	05	....	13	28.78	......	28.67	....	04	W.	S.W.	S.W.	1	3	3	10 S.	N.	N.	Light fall of snow.
„ „	15	14	....	10	28.54	......	28.05	....	09	N.E.	N.E.	0	3	3	0	10 S.	N.	0	Heavy snow storm during day.
„ „	16	05	....	15	28.62	......	28.45	....	05	N.W.	N.W.	0	5	5	0	0	5 K.S.	0	
„ „	17	17	....	....	28.53	......	......	....	22	0	0	0	0	0	0	Haze.	Haze.	Haze.	Thermometers abandoned.
„ „	18	....	....	....	......	......	......	....	....	0	0	0	0	0	0	0	0	0	Barometer broken by frost.
Lake Mistassini	19	....	....	....	......	......	......	....	....	0	0	0	0	0	0	0	0	0	Coldest night yet.
„ „	20	....	....	....	......	......	......	....	....	E.	E.	E.	1	1	1	10 S.	10 S.	10 S.	Colder than yesterday.
„ „	21	....	....	....	......	......	......	....	....	E.	E.	E.	1	1	1	10 S.	N.	10 S.	Light snow in afternoon.
„ „	22	....	....	....	......	......	......	....	....	E.	E.	S.	3	4	5	10 S.	N.	10 S.	3 in. snow during night and day.
„ „	23	....	....	....	......	......	......	....	....	N.W.	N.W.	N.W.	4	4	4	0	0	0	
H. B. Post Lake Mistassini	24	....	....	28	......	......	......	....	....	0	0	0	0	0	0	0	0	0	
„ „ „	25	....	....	....	......	......	......	....	....	0	0	0	0	0	0	0	0	0	
„ „ „	26	....	....	....	......	......	......	....	....	W.	W.	W.	1	2	1	0	0	0	
„ „ „	27	....	....	....	......	......	......	....	....	W.	W.	W.	1	1	1	0	0	N.	Light snow.
„ „ „	28	....	....	....	......	......	......	....	....	E.	S.E.	S.E.	2	1	1	N.	10 S.	10 S.	Light snow and rain.
„ „ „	29	....	....	....	......	......	......	....	....	S.W.	S.W.	S.W.	1	1	1	N.	N.	N.	Raining hard all day.
„ „ „	30	....	....	....	......	......	......	....	....	W.	W.	W.	3	3	3	0	0	0	
„ „ „	31	....	....	....	......	......	......	....	....	W.	W.	......	2	3	...	0	3	0	

Locality.	Date	Thermometer. 7	Thermometer. 2	Thermometer. 9	Barometer. 7	Barometer. 2	Barometer. 9	Maximum.	Minimum.	Wind. Direction. 7	Wind. Direction. 2	Wind. Direction. 9	Wind. Force. 7	Wind. Force. 2	Wind. Force. 9	Weather 7	Weather 2	Weather 9	Remarks.
	Jan.																		
H. B. Post Lake Mistassini	1			....	....	....	....	....	..	....	W.	....		3		....	0	....	
" " "	2	..		..	......	....	.....		....	E.	E.	E.	3	3	3	N.	N.	N.	6 inches of snow.
" " "	3	....	....	...	..	....	.....		..	E.	E.	E.	2	1	3	N.	N.	N.	Light snow flurries.
" " "	4	..	....		....	....	....	..		E.	S.	E.	1	1	3	0	5 K.S	N.	Snow falling in evening.
" " "	5	..	....	..	......	....		..	....	S.	E.	E.	3	3	3	N.	N.	N.	Snowing lightly all day.
" " "	6	...		...	..	....	....		...	....	....	....				....	....	....	
" " "	7	...	..	..	....	....	....		..	....	....	....				......	....	....	
" " "	8	.		.	...	....	...	..	...	....	.	..				......	....	....	
" " "	9	.		..	...	....	....	..	.	..	....	....				.	......	.	
" " "	10		....	...	...		.....	....	...	....	..	....				.		..	
" " "	11	....	.	.	...	......	..	..	.	....	...	....				....	....	..	
" " "	12	..		..	...		28 07	..	..	E.	W.	N.	3	4	5	0	0	0	
" " "	13	34	25	38	28 90	28 50	28 57	10	34	N W	N W.	N W.	1	4	3	0	0	0	
" " "	14	19	04	19	28 50	28 47	28 50	03	39	S.E.	W.	W.	1	4	1	0	N.	0	
" " "	15	40	10	09	28 66	28 55	28 50	04	40	0	E.	0	0	1	0	5 S.	10 S.	0	
" " "	16	15	13	19	28 52	28 58	28 58	06	16	0	W.	0	0	1	0	Haze.	Haze.	Haze.	
" " "	17	03	00	03	28 65	27 64	27 68	01	27	E.	E.	N.	3	4	5	N.	N.	0	1 inch of snow
" " "	18	29	20	11	28 20	28 29	28 37	21	29	N W.	N W.	0	4	3	0	0	0	0	
" " "	19	53	27	45	28 39	28 39	28 05	25	56	0	0	0	0	0	0	0	0	0	
" " "	20	19	06	00	28 37	28 20	28 21	00	52	S.E.	S.E.	E.	3	3	3	10 S.	N.	N.	Commenced snowing at 11 a.m.
" " "	21	01	10	25	28 24	28 00	28 18	01	06	E.	N W.	N W.	3	4	1	N.	10 S.	0	Stopped " "
" " "	22	36	19	37	28 55	28 12	28 17	19	37	0	W.	0	0	3	0	0	0	0	
" " "	23	08	00	06		28 18	28 22	10	37	S.E.	S.E	S.E.	5	5	1	N	N.	0	Snow from 1 a.m. to 5 p.m.
" " "	24	00	14	12	28 28	28 00	28 06	15	07	0	E.	E.	0	1	3	0	N	N.	1 inch of snow
" " "	25	04	02	10	27 05	27 95	27 00	16		0	W.	0	0	1	0	0	0	0	
" " "	26	25	11	15	27 71	27 60	27 72	05	25	0	N.E.	N W	0	1	2	0	N.	N.	Light fall of snow.
" " "	27	30	31	45	28 00	28 25	28 11	0	10	N W	N W.	0	1	2	0	0	0	0	
" " "	28	56	23	40	28 46	28 38	28 25	26	56	0	0	E	0	0	1	0	0	0	
" " "	29	36	03	16	28 19	28 20	28 29	26		0	W.	0	0	.	0	0	N.	0	Snow flurries
" " "	30	13	02	18	28 31	28 30	28 30	03	21	E.	E.	0	1	1	0	0	0	0	
" " "	31	20	07	32	28 30	28 18	.. ..	03	29	S.W	W.	0	1	1	0	0	0	0	
	Feb.																		
" " "	1	22	14	18	28 40	28 30	28 30	03	38	W.	N.	N W.	1	1	3	N.	10 S.	10 S.	Light snow flurries.
" " "	2	31	18	25	28 30	28 25	28 25	11	31	N W	N W.	N W.	1	1	1	0	0	0	
" " "	3	35	13	26	28 25	28 15	28 10	18	41	0	N W	N W	1	1	1	0	0	0	
" " "	4	31	02	07	28 10	28 15	27 90	11	40	0	0	0	0	0	0	0	0	0	
" " "	5	05	04	10	27 86	28 00	28 65	08		0	N.	N	0	1	1	N	N	0	1 inch of snow
" " "	6	13	10	30	28 75	28 46	28 [illegible]	05	13	N W	N W	0	1	1	0	0	0	0	

H. B. Post Lake Mistassini	7	46	05	31	28.49	28.50	28.42	08	46	0	0	N.	0	0	1	0	0	0	
" " "	8	19	05	05	28.35	28.32	28.42	02	40	N.W.	N.	0	0	1	0	0	N.	0	Light fall of snow in p.m.
" " "	9	10	01	03	28.25	28.65	28.30	07	19	0	N.	N.	0	1	1	10 S.	0	0	
" " "	10	25	26	04	27.65	27.59	27.55	26	10	E.	E.	W.	5	5	3	N.	N.	N.	Snow all day, (6 inches.)
" " "	11	17	12	14	27.60	27.75	28.00	12	17	S.W.	W.	W.	3	4	3	0	0	0	
" " "	12	20	04	35	28.00	28.10	28.20	04	20	S.W.	S.W.	0	4	5	0	0	0	0	
" " "	13	42	04	25	28.29	28.39	28.30	04	42	0	S.	0	0	1	0	0	0	0	
" " "	14	15	06	10	28.45	28.49	28.45	06	25	E.	E.	0	2	3	0	0	0	0	
" " "	15	00	13	08	28.50	28.50	28.50	18	10	S.	E.	E.	3	3	3	10 S.	0	0	
" " "	16	10	21	20	28.50	28.35	28.29	32	10	E.	E.	E.	3	1	5	0	0	0	
" " "	17	15	21	12	28.10	28.00	28.00	35	15	E.	E.	E.	5	5	1	0	0	0	
" " "	18	00	21	13	28.22	28.20	28.20	21	00	E.	0	0	1	0	0	N.	N.	N.	S'w from 7 a.m. to 6 p.m. (6 in.)
" " "	19	09	15	10	28.20	28.10	28.10	33	09	0	N.	N.	1	2	3	10 S.	10 S.	10 S.	
" " "	20	13	23	19	28.10	28.10	28.15	34	09	W.	N.	N.	1	3	3	10 S.	N.	N.	3 inches of snow.
" " "	21	07	20	01	28.29	28.30	28.39	37	07	N.	N.	N.	1	2	2	10 S.	0	0	
" " "	22	06	08	03	28.40	28.40	28.45	09	06	N.	N.	N.	1	3	2	0	0	0	
" " "	23	15	.....	.....	28.55	.....	.....	10	15	N.	.....	.....	1	0	0	0	0	0	
" " "	24	.....	.....	.....	.....	.....	.....	.....	.....	0	.....	.....	0	.....	.....	.....	.....	.....	
" " "	25	.....	.....	.....	.....	.....	.....	.....	.....	.....	.....	.....	.....	.....	.....	.....	.....	.....	
" " "	26	10	25	25	28.30	28.20	28.20	25	10	E.	S.	S.	3	2	1	0	N.	N.	1 inch of snow.
" " "	27	22	28	20	28.25	28.20	28.25	32	22	0	0	0	0	0	0	N.	N.	N.	Light flurries of snow.
" " "	28	08	19	07	28.35	28.35	28.30	30	08	N.	0	0	1	0	0	N.	0	0	1 inch of snow.
	Mar.																		
" " "	1	24	30	22	28.10	28.00	28.00	....	....	E.	E.	E.	1	1	1	N.	N.	N.	Com'ced snowing 6 a.m. (1 in.)
" " "	2	15	18	08	28.00	27.95	28.00	....	....	N.	N.W.	N.	1	3	3	N.	N.	0	Stopped snowing 7 p.m. (2 in.)
" " "	3	17	17	06	28.15	28.26	28.22	....	....	E.	E.	E.	1	1	1	0	0	0	
" " "	4	03	26	15	28.20	28.25	28.23	....	....	E.	E.	0	1	1	0	0	10 S.	0	
" " "	5	02	....	09	28.32	.....	28.50	....	....	N.	.....	N.	1	..	3	N.	.....	0	
" " "	6	24	04	20	28.48	28.49	28.50	....	....	0	N.E.	N.	0	1	1	0	0	0	
" " "	7	35	02	22	28.49	28.50	28.50	....	....	0	N.E.	0	0	2	0	0	0	0	
" " "	8	27	06	23	28.49	28.10	28.35	....	....	0	N.	E.	0	2	1	0	0	0	
" " "	9	31	10	05	28.30	27.95	27.90	....	....	E.	E.	E.	1	3	3	0	0	N.	Commenced snowing at 4 p.m.
" " "	10	12	08	15	28.00	28.20	28.35	....	....	0	N.W.	N.W.	0	3	3	0	N.	0	
" " "	11	30	11	31	28.40	28.45	28.32	....	....	0	0	E.	0	0	3	0	0	N.	
" " "	12	31	03	05	28.55	24.60	28.63	....	....	N.	N.W.	0	3	3	0	0	0	0	
" " "	13	08	16	12	28.62	28.50	28.40	....	....	E.	E.	E.	1	3	1	0	0	0	
" " "	14	10	18	....	28.30	28.30	.....	....	....	0	0	0	0	0	0	0	0	0	
" " "	15	01	06	10	28.00	27.80	.....	....	....	E.	E.	.....	1	1	..	N.	N.	N.	Commenced snowing last night.
" " "	16	22	04	11	28.00	28.00	28.15	....	....	W.	W.	W.	1	2	3	0	0	.....	Stopped " " (2 in.)
" " "	17	22	04	10	28.22	28.22	28.28	....	....	W.	S.W.	0	1	3	0	0	0	0	
" " "	18	19	09	15	28.30	28.30	28.32	....	....	0	S.	.....	0	1	..	0	0	0	
" " "	19	25	11	....	28.29	28.20	.....	....	....	0	N.	.....	0	1	..	0	10 S.	.....	
" " "	20	01	07	....	27.72	27.75	.....	....	....	N.	N.	.....	3	3	..	N.	N.	.....	Commenced snowing last night.
" " "	21	11	03	10	27.90	28.00	28.20	....	....	N.	N.	N.W.	3	2	3	0	0	0	Stop'd snowi'g last night, (2 in.)
" " "	22	18	07	18	28.38	28.39	28.42	....	....	N.W.	N.W.	E.	3	2	1	0	0	0	
" " "	23	22	13	05	28.45	28.39	28.29	....	....	E.	S.	E.	1	1	1	0	0	0	
" " "	24	12	22	02	28.20	28.20	28.25	....	....	E.	S.	N.	1	1	1	0	N.	0	Light snow in middle of day.

* The readings following are taken with an Aneroid Barometer.

LOCALITY.	Date	Thermometer.			Barometer.			Maximum.	Minimum.	Wind. Direction.			Wind. Force.			Weather.			Remarks.
	Mar.	7	2	9	7	2	9			7	2	9	7	2	9	7	2	9	
H. B. Post Lake Mistassini	25	21	12	09	28 32	28 32	28 30	....	....	E.	W.	0	1	3	0	0	0	0	
" " "	26	01	21	05	28.22	28 25	28.30	....	....	S.	W.	0	1	1	0	0	0	0	
" " "	27	10	31	15	28.20	28 00	28 15	....	....	S.E.	W.	W.	1	3	3	0	10 S.	0	
" " "	28	03	08	23	28.28	28 35	28 16	....	....	N.	N. W.	0	3	2	0	0	0	0	
" " "	29	20	12	10	28 50	28 50	28 50	....	....	0	E	0	2	1	0	0	0	0	
" " "	30	03	27	10	28 40	28 42	28 40	....	....	E.	E	E.	3	3	1	0	0	0	
" " "	31	25		27	28.25	.....	28 20	....	....	E.	.....	0	1		0	N.	.....	10 S.	Snow 3 inches.
	April.																		
" " "	1	30	13		28 10	28 30	.....		...	W.	N.	.....	5	5		N.	0	.....	Snow.
" " "	2	04	21	01	28 50	28 50	28 50	....	....	W.	S.	0	1	2	0	0	0	0	
" " "	3	09	22		28 60	28 60	.....	....	....	0	N.	.....	0	1		0	0	...	
" " "	4	00	32	20	28.40	28 40	28 20	....	....	0	E	E.	0	1	1	0	0	0	
" " "	5	22	31	22	27 80	27 80	27 80	....	....	W.	E	0	1	2	0	0	0	0	
" " "	6	21	36	21	28 28	28 28	28 45	....	....	N.	N.	N.	1	3	1	0	0	0	
" " "	7	24	39	...	28 50	.....	...	....	...	E.	E	.....	1	3		10 S.	0	.....	
" " "	8	36		09	28 00	.....	28 12	..	...	S.	.....	W.	1		5	N.	...	N.	Rain and snow.
" " "	9	01	19	06	28.22	28 32	28 32	..	..	N.	N.	N.	3	3	2	0	0	0	
" " "	10	23	30	25	28 26	28 22	28 22	....	..	E.	W.	0	2	1	0	0	0	0	
" " "	11	...	...		...	..	.....	....	...	.....	...	.....				.....	...	..	
" " "	12	..	..	..	..	...	..	...	..	...	...	...				...	.....	...	
" " "	13	07	25	15	28 39	28 40	22 11	..	....	N.	N.	N.	3	3	1	0	0	0	
" " "	14	08	31		28 50	28 50	.....	...	...	N.	N.	.....	1	2		0	0	.....	
" " "	15	10	30	..	28 12	28 40	.....	..	...	N.	N.	.....	2	3		0	0	..	
" " "	16	24	30	28	28 40	28 40	28 40	...	.	N.	N.	N.	3	3	1	10 S.	0	0	
" " "	17	25	38	28	28 62	28 65	28 80	...	.	N.	N.	N.	3	2	1	0	0	0	
" " "	18	19	42	25	28 76	28 78	28 71			0	N	N.	0	1	1	0	0	0	
" " "	19	35	51	35	28 75	28.70	28 62	...	..	0	N.	E	0	1	1	0	0	...	
" " "	20	15	11	37	28 60	28 55	28 60		..	E.	W.	N.	1	1	1	0	N.	0	Rain.
" " "	21	22	30	35	28 62	28 62	28 62		....	N.	N.	0	1	1	0	0	0	10 S.	
" " "	22	36	47	47	28 50	28 48	28 38		.	E	S.	E	1	2	3	N.	0	0	Rain.
" " "	23	15	60	45	28 28	29 32	28 35	..		E.	S.	S.	1	3	1	0	0	N.	Rain.
" " "	24	35	37	16	28 40	28 45	28 45	..	..	N.	N.	N.	1	1	1	0	0	...	
" " "	25	18	32	23	28 62	28 62	28 65	..		N.	N.	N.	1	3	1	0	0	0	
" " "	26	28	40	33	28 50	28 50	28 40	.	.	E.	E	E.	1	2	1	0	0	0	
" " "	27	34	35	34	28 30	28 28	28 30			N.	N.	W.	1	1	3	N.	N.	N.	Snow.
" " "	28	22	36	26	28 38	28 30	28 32	..	...	N.	N.	N.	3	1	1	N.	10 S.	0	Snow.
" " "	29	28		...	.....	.....	.....			E.	....	..	1			0	...	...	
" " "	30	31	....		28 12	.....	.....	....	..	N. W.	.....	.....	1	...		10 S.	.....	.....	

	May																		
H. B. Post Lake Mistassini	1	20	25	18	28.31	28.31	28.39	30	16	N.	N.	N.	3	1	1	N.	0	0	Snow in morning.
" " "	2	10	21	....	28.40	28.40	......	40	11	N.	N.	......	1	2	...	0	0	......	
" " "	3	19	29	25	28.28	28.24	28.24	30	08	N.	N.W.	0	3	3	0	0	0	0	
" " "	4	40	48	37	28.25	28.25	28.34	48	12	S.	S.E.	N.	1	3	1	0	0	0	
" " "	5	36	17	....	28.42	28.44	......	49	15	0	E.	......	0	1	...	0	0	......	
" " "	6	38	48	40	28.40	28.40	28.40	51	23	E.	E.	S.	3	3	1	10 S.	10 S.	10 S.	
" " "	7	38	18	....	28.38	28.30	......	51	27	E.	E.	......	3	3	...	10 S.	0	......	
" " "	8	37	47	....	28.30	28.28	......	57	35	E.	S.	......	1	2	...	10 S.	N.	......	Rain.
" " "	9	30	45	33	28.20	28.16	28.16	51	33	W.	0	N.	1	0	1	10 S.	0	0	
" " "	10	41	45	35	28.09	28.04	28.04	47	29	N.	W.	N.	2	2	1	0	N.	0	Rain.
" " "	11	33	39	....	28.20	28.29	......	36	28	W.	W.	......	3	3	...	0	10 S.	......	
" " "	12	....	....	....	......	......	......	42	23	E.	......	......	3	...	...	0	......	......	
" " "	13	43	....	....	28.44	......	......	47	37	0	......	......	0	...	...	0	......	......	
" " "	14	51	60	....	28.40	28.38	......	56	36	W.	W.	......	3	3	...	0	5 K.S.	......	
" " "	15	....	40	....	28.54	......	......	61	28	N.	N.	......	3	2	...	0	......	......	
" " "	16	....	66	....	......	28.27	......	...	29	S.W.	S.W.	S.W.	3	3	1	10 S.	10 S.	10 S.	
" " "	17	55	47	....	28.24	28.28	......	69	41	N.	N.	......	3	2	...	10 S.	10 S.	......	Showers during day.
" " "	18	30	....	....	28.48	......	......	55	31	N.	......	......	1	...	...	10 S.	......	......	
" " "	19	34	....	....	28.46	......	......	57	23	N.	......	......	3	...	...	0	......	......	
" " "	20	....	....	....	28.60	......	......	55	23	N.W.	......	......	1	...	...	......	......	......	
" " "	21	55	....	....	28.61	......	......	67	27	E.	......	......	1	...	...	0	......	......	
" " "	22	41	....	....	28.50	......	......	52	35	S.	S.W.	S.W.	1	1	1	10 S.	Haze	......	
" " "	23	40	....	....	28.45	......	......	73	31	S.W.	......	......	1	...	...	0	......	......	
" " "	24	73	....	....	28.38	......	......	80	37	W.	......	......	3	...	...	0	......	......	
" " "	25	45		....	28.26	......	......	85	41	S.	......	......	3	...	...	N.	......	......	Rain showers during day.
" " "	26	44	51	....	28.20	28.30	......	75	43	W.	W.	......	3	4	...	10 S.	10 S.	......	Rain showers during day.
" " "	27	....	40	....	......	28.55	......	...	...	W.	W.	......	3	3	...	10 S.	10 S.	......	
" " "	28	....	....	54	......	......	28.50	...	29	N.W.	N.W.	0	3	3	...	0	0	0	
" " "	29	53	67	50	28.46	28.43	28.41	61	30	N.W.	N.	......	1	3	...	0	5 K.S.	0	
" " "	30	51	73	63	28.37	28.33	28.30	61	31	......	S.E.	S.E.	...	1	3	0	5 K.S.	5 K.S.	
" " "	31	59	67	50	28.31	28.22	28.25	75	46	S.E.	S.E.	S.E.	1	4	4	Haze	Haze	10 S.	Began to rain at 5.30 p.m.
	June.																		
" " "	1	45	46	46	28.10	28.10	28.21	68	44	E.	E.	E.	3	4	3	10 S.	10 S.	10 S.	Rained all day.
" " "	2	40	52	48	28.30	28.39	28.40	50	38	E.	E.	0	1	2	0	10 S.	10 S.	10 S.	Showers during day.
" " "	3	46	60	60	28.31	28.25	28.31	58	38	S.E.	W.	N.W.	3	4	3	10 S.	7 K.S.	10 S.	Showers during morning.
" " "	4	35	50	40	28.38	28.37	28.39	61	35	N.W.	N.	N.	3	2	1	10 S.	5 K.S.	Clear.	Light flurry of snow at 4.30 a.m.
" " "	5	38	50	43	28.42	28.37	28.39	56	30	0	N.	0	0	1	0	10 S.	7 K.S.	3 K.S.	Light showers all day.
" " "	6	49	....	52	28.40	......	28.31	50	32	0	......	E.	0	...	1	0	3 K.S.	9 S.	Heavy rain in a.m. with snow.
" " "	7	50	48	40	28.13	27.09	28.05	70	40	S.E.	S.E.	N.W.	5	5	4	10 S.	10 S.	10 S.	Flurries snow during day ½ in.
" " "	8	35	45	35	27.98	27.87	27.91	52	35	S.	S.E.	N.W.	3	4	3	10 S.	10 S.	10 S.	
" " "	9	35	46	40	28.14	28.24	28.30	51	32	N.W.	N.W.	W.	3	3	3	10 S.	10 S.	5 K.S.	
" " "	10	45	57	52	28.46	28.47	28.48	46	32	N.W.	N.W.	0	1	1	0	0	5 K.S.	2 K.S.	Light showers during the night
" " "	11	55	68	58	28.48	28.50	28.49	61	32	0	S.W.	0	0	1	0	5 K.S.	0	0	
" " "	12	54	62	54	28.41	28.37	28.30	70	39	S.	S.	S.	2	5	3	5 K.S.	10 S.	10 S.	Rain at 2 p.m.
" " "	13	58	68	57	28.08	28.18	28.18	70	52	W.	W.	0	1	2	0	10 S.	3 S.	5 S.	Stopped raining at 11 a.m.
" " "	14	45	65	60	28.15	28.23	28.32	75	45	N.	N.W.	0	1	1	0	10 S.	5 S.	0	Rain from 12.30 a.m. to 8 a.m.
" " "	15	57	71	62	28.40	28.37	28.20	67	37	E.	S.	S.	1	1	1	0	8 S.	5 S.	
" " "	16	65	60	42	28.10	28.16	28.25	76	55	S.W.	W.	N.W.	1	4	4	10 S.	8 S.	8 S.	Light showers during night.

LOCALITY.	Date	Thermometer.			Barometer.			Maximum.	Minimum.	Wind. Direction.			Wind. Force.			Weather.			Remarks.
	June.	7	2	9	7	2	9			7	2	9	7	2	9	7	2	9	
H. B. Post Lake Mistassini	17	40	65	.	28 30	28 27	.	71	38	S. W.	S.W.	.....	1	4		10 S	8 S	.....	Light rain during afternoon.
" " "	18	....	58	40	.....	28 40	28 49	68	39	...	W.	N. E.		1	1	.....	10 S	5 S	" " night.
" " "	19	46	65	54	28 50	28 48	28 50	60	30	S. E.	N. W.	0	1	1	0	0	5 S	0	Aurora (2) last night
" " "	20	50	67	55	28 50	28 41	28 40	72	40	S. E.	S.	S.	1	1	1	0	8 S	10 S	Rain from 5 p.m. to 10 p.m.
" " "	21	57	72	65	28 30	28 20	28 11	70	48	S.	S.	S.	2	4	1	0	Haze	10 S	Rain 3 p.m.
" " "	22	45	45	41	28 08	27 99	28 12	77	47	W.	N. W.	S. W.	3	2	3	10 S	10 S	5 S	Rain all day.
" " "	23	40	44	38	28 00	28 00	28 14	50	35	W.	N. W.	N. W.	4	4	1	10 S	10 S	10 S	Light sho'ers rain & sno' all d'y
" " "	24	46	71	50	28 2	28 22	28 31	48	65	S.	W.	W.	1	3	1	10 S	5 K S	5 K S	Showers during night and day.
" " "	25	65	73	65	28 3	28 31	28 31	74	47	W.	W.	0	1	3	0	0	8 K S	0	Thunder shower in p.m.
" " "	26	65	75	62	28 41	28 45	28 41	79	57	0	N. W.	0	0	1	0	0	5 K S	0	" " a.m.
" " "	27	60	70	62	28 37	28 53	28 35	78	52	S.	W.	N. W.	2	3	1	8 K S	5 K S	8 K S	Heavy thunder showers.
" " "	28	43	52	47	28 51	28 45	28 49	77	38	N.	W.	N.	1	1	1	5 K S	5 K S	8 K S	
" " "	29	46	...	....	28 41	.....	......	53	38	N.		...	1			5 K S	.	...	
" " "	30	....	...	....	.....	...	.....	....		..		.....		..		.....	.....		
	July.																		
" " "	1	49	57	55	....	.	......	53	40	N. E.	N. E.	N. E.	1	1	1	10 S	N.	N.	
" " "	2	56	66	62	.....	..	......	68	49	N. E.	N. W.	E.	1	2	1	5 K S	9 K	5 K	
" " "	3	60	74	60	....	.....	...	77	51	E.	N. E.	E.	1	2	1	7 K S	5 K S	5 K	
" " "	4	60	76	59	.....	.....	...	76	53	E.	S. E.	S. E.	1	2	1	10 S	5 K S	5 K S	
" " "	5	66	73	64	...	..	...	76	51	S. E.	S.	S.	1	4	1	0	10 S	5 K	
" " "	6	63	77	68	.....	.....	.....	74	58	S. E.	S.	S.	1	2	1	10 S	0	0	
" " "	7	60	70	66	.....	....	.....	74	61	S. E.	S. E.	S.	3	5	1	0	N.	7 K S	
" " "	8	68		61	.	.....	.....	71	62	S.		S.	3	3	1	0	.	7 S	
" " "	9	64	69	58	....	....	....	72	58	S. W.	W.	N. W.	3	4	3	5 K	5 K	7 K S	
" " "	10	42	51	48	...	...	...	72	41	N. W.	N. W.	N.	4	2	1	10 S	9 K	0	
" " "	11	52	70	58		.	...	61	39	S. W.	W.	N.	1	4	1	7 S	5 K S	0	
" " "	12	61	71	64	....	..	....	71	44	S. W.	S. W.	S.	1	3	1	0	7 K S	0	
" " "	13	65	79	64	....	....	...	..	60	S. W.	S.	S.	3	4	3	5 K	7 S	0	
" " "	14	46	52	51	.....	.....	......	...	46	N.	N.	N. W.	3	2	1	N.	N.	N.	
" " "	15	50	66	57	.....	....	......	51	49	N. W.	N. W.	W.	2	3	1	10 S	5 K	7 K S	
" " "	16	57	71	68	.....	....	....	66	48	S. W.	S. W.	S. W.	1	5	1	7 K S	8 K S	10 S	
" " "	17	66	72	49	.....	.....	....	75	59	S.	W.	N. W.	3	5	3	N.	7 S	10 S	
" " "	18	45	60	53	.	....	.....	72	39	N. W.	N. W.	N. W.	3	2	1	7 S	7 S	0	
" " "	19	56	58	55	.....	......	.....	69	46	S. W.	S.	N. W.	1	1	1	N.	N.	10 S	
" " "	20	58	76	55	.....	...	.	57	45	N.	E.	E.	1	1	1	10 S	5 K	5 K	
" " "	21	59	76	57	......	..	......	...	51	E.	N. W.	W.	1	1	1	5 K	7 S	7 K S	
" " "	22	51	62	50	....	..	......	....	50	N.	N. W.	N.	3	2	1	10 S	8 K S	0	
" " "	23	63	....	....	.....	....	......	70	46	S.	.....	.....	1	.		0	....	....	

H. B. Post Lake Mistassini	24	...	...	...	...	...	...	76	...	...	...	...	...	...	...	...	...	...	
" " "	25	...	...	...	...	...	...	...	...	...	...	...	...	...	...	...	...	...	
" " "	26	...	...	...	...	...	...	...	...	...	...	...	...	...	...	...	...	...	
" " "	27	...	...	...	...	...	...	...	...	...	...	...	...	...	...	...	...	...	
" " "	28	...	...	...	...	...	...	...	...	...	...	...	...	...	...	...	...	...	
" " "	29	...	...	...	...	...	...	...	...	...	...	...	...	...	...	...	...	...	
" " "	30	...	...	...	...	...	...	...	...	...	...	...	...	...	...	...	...	...	
" " "	31	...	...	...	...	...	...	...	...	...	...	...	...	...	...	...	...	...	
	Aug.																		
" " "	1	48	60	53	28.49	28.50	28.50	61	41	0	N.W.	0	0	1	0	8 K.S.	10 S.	0	Rain from 7.30 a.m. to 4 p.m.
" " "	2	51	68	51	28.66	28.60	28.65	65	31	0	S.	0	0	1	0	0	0	0	
" " "	3	54	72	65	28.50	28.43	28.41	75	43	S.E.	S.E.	S.E.	1	5	3	0	0	5 K.S.	Aurora (2).
" " "	4	54	61	62	28.20	28.02	28.06	74	52	S.E.	S.E.	S.E.	5	5	3	10 S.	10 S.	10 S.	Began to rain at 2 a.m.
" " "	5	46	45	44	28.21	28.40	28.52	74	46	W.	N.W.	N.W.	3	2	1	10 S.	10 S.	8 K.S.	Ceased raining at 4 p.m.
" " "	6	47	65	50	28.64	28.64	28.66	50	33	0	N.E.	0	0	1	0	0	5 K.S.	0	Frost on low ground.
" " "	7	51	65	50	28.65	28.65	28.59	65	38	0	S.E.	0	0	3	0	0	0	0	Aurora (3).
" " "	8	55	75	63	28.55	28.64	28.58	72	45	0	S.	S.	0	3	1	0	0	0	Aurora (3). Began rain 6 p.m.
" " "	9	60	71	72	28.56	28.46	28.42	75	52	S.	S.	S.	3	3	1	3 K.S.	7 K.S.	10 S.	Showers during a.m.
" " "	10	53	65	62	28.46	28.51	28.52	73	53	N.W.	N.	0	1	1	0	10 S.	3 K.S.	0	
" " "	11	58	...	61	28.52	...	28.49	68	52	0	...	0	0	...	0	0	...	5 K.S.	Aurora (3). Showers till 3 p.m.
" " "	12	62	68	62	28.50	28.44	28.41	81	52	0	0	0	0	0	0	10 S.	10 S.	3 K.S.	
" " "	13	61	74	65	28.31	28.21	28.14	73	53	S.	S.	S.	3	3	1	0	7 K.S.	10 S.	Began to rain at 5 p.m.
" " "	14	55	44	46	28.04	28.12	28.19	72	53	N.W.	N.W.	N.W.	3	4	1	10 S.	10 S.	8 K.S.	Stopped raining at 4.30 p.m.
" " "	15	48	59	52	28.29	28.37	28.41	58	42	0	S.W.	0	0	3	0	8 K.S.	5 K.S.	8 K.S.	Showers during the night.
" " "	16	51	71	62	28.51	28.54	28.46	63	41	S.W.	S.W.	S.W.	1	2	1	7 K.S.	5 K.S.	10 S.	" "
" " "	17	56	72	60	28.52	28.39	28.39	72	50	S.W.	S.W.	S.W.	1	1	1	8 K.S.	5 K.S.	7 K.S.	Rain 3 a.m. to 11 a.m.
" " "	18	56	74	60	28.31	28.21	28.18	74	56	S.W.	S.W.	S.W.	1	1	1	10 S.	8 K.S.	7 K.S.	Showers during night and day.
" " "	19	51	49	42	28.16	28.19	28.31	74	51	W.	N.W.	0	3	3	0	8 K.S.	10 S.	0	" " "
" " "	20	50	55	48	28.36	28.41	28.44	52	39	W.	W.	0	3	3	0	0	10 S.	0	" " "
" " "	21	52	55	...	28.50	28.46	...	60	37	S.E.	S.	...	3	4	...	5 K.S.	10 S.	...	Rain showers during day.
" " "	22	...	...	...	...	...	...	...	...	...	...	...	...	...	...	...	...	...	
" " "	23	...	...	...	...	...	...	...	...	...	...	...	...	...	...	...	...	...	
" " "	24	...	...	...	...	...	...	...	...	...	...	...	...	...	...	...	...	...	
" " "	25	...	...	...	...	...	...	...	...	...	...	...	...	...	...	...	...	...	
" " "	26	...	...	...	...	...	...	...	...	...	...	...	...	...	...	...	...	...	
" " "	27	...	...	...	...	...	...	...	...	...	...	...	...	...	...	...	...	...	
" " "	28	...	...	...	...	...	...	...	...	...	...	...	...	...	...	...	...	...	
" " "	29	...	...	...	...	...	...	...	...	...	...	...	...	...	...	...	...	...	
" " "	30	...	...	...	...	...	...	...	...	...	...	...	...	...	...	...	...	...	
" " "	31	...	...	...	...	...	...	...	...	...	...	...	...	...	...	...	...	...	

www.ingramcontent.com/pod-product-compliance
Lightning Source LLC
Chambersburg PA
CBHW031802090426
42739CB00008B/1126
9783337329945